Kingdom Scroll

Other Books by David Edgren

Books in the Adventures in the Bible series
The Serpent Scroll
The Lamb Scroll

Other kids books
Giant Boots

Adult books
The NEW Church
28 Stories

The Kingdom Scroll

Adventures in the Bible

DAVID EDGREN

Pacific Press® Publishing Association
Nampa, Idaho
Oshawa, Ontario, Canada
www.pacificpress.com

Cover design by Gerald Lee Monks
Cover illustration by Marcus Mashburn
Inside design by Aaron Troia

Copyright © 2011 by Pacific Press® Publishing Association
Printed in the United States of America
All rights reserved

Some character dialogue and Scripture quotations marked NLT are taken from the Holy Bible, New Living Translation, copyright © 1996, 2004. Used by permission of Tyndale House Publishers, Inc., Wheaton, Illinois 60189. All rights reserved.

The author assumes full responsibility for the accuracy of all facts and quotations as cited in this book.

You can obtain additional copies of this book by calling toll-free 1-800-765-6955 or by visiting http://www.adventistbookcenter.com.

Library of Congress Cataloging-in-Publication Data:
Edgren, David, 1972-
The kingdom scroll / David Edgren.
   p. cm. — (Adventures in the Bible)
ISBN 13: 978-0-8163-2483-5 (pbk.)
ISBN 10: 0-8163-2483-2 (pbk.)
1. Kingdom of God—Biblical teaching—Juvenile literature. 2. Bible—Study and teaching. 3. Bible stories, English. I. Title. II. Series.
BS680.K52E35 2011
231.7'2—dc22

                                              2011003634

11 12 13 14 15 • 5 4 3 2 1

Dedication

This book is dedicated to

Rachael Hannah,
Michael James,
and
Cyrus Paul

My inspiration!
The kingdom is truly alive in each of you.
Love,
Dad

Table of Contents

Chapter 1   Into the Bible 9

Chapter 2   The Great Controversy 15

Chapter 3   A Loud Speech 20

Chapter 4   A Kingdom Dream 24

Chapter 5   A Palace Appearing 29

Chapter 6   With All Respect 33

Chapter 7   Following Daniel 38

Chapter 8   A Dream Revealed 43

Chapter 9   Kingdom After Kingdom 47

Chapter 10   Kingdom Stones 52

Chapter 11   Five Stones 57

Chapter 12   Two Stone Slabs 62

Chapter 13 A Stone's Throw 67

Chapter 14 Kingdom Builders 71

Chapter 15 Retracing Steps 76

Chapter 16 Together Again 81

Chapter 17 Bow or Burn 86

Chapter 18 Frozen Worship 91

Chapter 19 Kingdom Children 96

Chapter 20 One-Foot Law 102

Chapter 21 God's Storyteller 107

Chapter 22 Kingdom Stories 112

Chapter 23 Hidden Treasure 117

Chapter 24 God's Kingdom 122

Chapter 1
Into the Bible

As the kids finished their lunch, Dad looked at each one of them with pride. "You three have really been enjoying Paul's new Bible, haven't you?"

"It's awesome!" James, always the first to get a word in, answered with a smile.

Hannah, the youngest of the three, added, "Dad, it's the coolest thing ever. We go right into the middle of the stories—like they're all around us!"

Dad looked at Paul. "Is this some kind of game you three have created?"

Paul shook his head slowly from side to side, chewing and swallowing the last bite of his sandwich. "No, Dad," he answered, "Grandpa Wesley says it's a special Bible."

"All Bibles are special," Dad said.

"Not this special," James said with a laugh. "Have you ever been sucked into one of your Bibles?"

"'Sucked in'?" Dad questioned. "Do you mean drawn into or something else? Usually, 'sucked in' means you've been tricked by someone into doing something. Surely, the Bible isn't tricking you. What do you mean?"

"You know when you pull the plug at the bottom of the bathtub?" James asked, biting a slice of apple in two. "The water gets sucked into the drain. That's what happened to us!"

Dad was struggling to understand. "So you have been reading the Bible in the bathtub?"

All three of the kids laughed. James tried to say something, but he was laughing so hard he snorted instead, which caused everyone to laugh even harder.

Paul regained his composure first and said, "The special Bible Grandpa Wesley gave me for my birthday yesterday actually pulls us inside of it. We go right into the stories."

"That's impossible," Dad said. "You must be imagining it!"

"It seems pretty real," Hannah said. "I don't think my imagination is that good."

"And we are all imagining the same thing," James said, "because we are all together in the same stories. Whenever we finish one story, we leave together and arrive in the next story. And we don't even know what story it is until we've guessed it out."

" 'Guessed it out'?" Dad echoed.

"Yeah," Paul said, holding his hand up to quiet James. "*The Prophet Kids' Bible* came with four scroll cards. They are maps that are activated by touching a red word in the Bible. Once we have fully explored one story, another one appears on the card. We all touch the card at the same time, and that sends us zipping into another story."

"But it's all white!" James cut in.

"White?" Dad asked.

"Yes," James continued. "There is nothing on the page until we guess the right words. And when we say the right words, those things appear—until we know where we are and someone says the name of that story—then everything appears and the story starts!"

"But, we are only watching," Hannah explained, "like a movie. We can't change anything."

Into the Bible

"Why not?" Dad asked, playing along.

"Because!" James shouted. "It's the Bible! You can't go changing the Bible! It's God's Word!"

"True," Dad said. He was enjoying this. "So, let me see if I've got this right." He lifted his hand in the air and pointed one finger to the ceiling. "You point your finger like this, then put it on the scroll card like this." Dad lowered his finger to the table. "And then, *kerpow*, you're gone. And *shazam*, you're on a blank page, ready to start exploring?"

"Yes!" all three said together.

Hannah clapped her hands with joy, "You understand now!"

"He's just being silly," James said. "Aren't you, Dad?"

"Well," Dad said thoughtfully, "I am really glad you guys are exploring the Bible. And if making a game out of it makes it more fun, then I'm all for it!"

"Yep," James said, crossing his arms. "He thinks we're making it all up!"

"Not all of it," Dad argued. "You three have definitely been deep into the Bible because the stories you have told me each time you come out of the boys' room are definitely real Bible stories. So, you are certainly exploring the Bible. And it sounds like you are having lots of fun doing it!"

"We sure are," Paul said.

"So," Dad asked, "of the stories you've explored so far, which has been your favorite?"

Hannah answered first. "I liked seeing Adam and Eve get married. That was beautiful! Did you know Adam sang Eve a song at their wedding?"

Dad raised his eyebrows. "Really?" he asked.

"It's written as a poem in the Bible," Paul explained. "But when we saw it, Adam sang it."

"Fantastic!" Dad said, "Don't tell your mother. She'll expect me to sing a song on our anniversary!"

Everyone laughed. "You can sing," Hannah said. "I've heard you!"

Dad cleared his throat loudly, "What about you, Paul; what's your favorite story so far?"

Paul smiled. "Good save, Dad." He paused and thought about it for a second and then said, "I think when we saw Abraham and Isaac find the ram caught by its horns. They were so relieved!"

"A lot of people struggle with that story," Dad said.

"Why?" James asked.

"Because it talks about a father willing to kill his son," Dad said, leaning back in his chair. "That should make every reader concerned! Many people think we shouldn't let kids hear that story!"

"But it's just like what God did," Hannah said seriously, "when He sent His Son, Jesus, to die for us."

"Yes," Dad agreed. "But it's still a very hard lesson. To be willing to give God whatever He asks is a difficult thing when a tough challenge comes along."

"Isaac was willing," Paul added. "He didn't understand God's demand, but he wanted everything to go God's way."

"*Hmmm*," Dad said, lost in thought.

"Would you do it, Dad?" James asked. "If God asked you to sacrifice one of us?"

"I don't think I could," Dad said. "You are all so special to me."

"Yeah," James said, "not me for sure. Maybe Paul?"

"James!" Paul and Dad said in unison. They looked at James and saw the impish grin on his face and everyone laughed, breaking the tension in the room. James had a unique ability to use humor to help people relax.

"Wow!" Dad said, expelling all the air in his lungs. "You guys are really challenging me today! First, I'm supposed to learn to sing love songs to Mom. Now, you've got me thinking about how hard it can be to obey God."

"That's what these Bible studies have been doing to us," Paul said, "challenging us to think."

"And making us ride an emotional yo-yo!" James added.

"James, what about you?" Dad asked. "What Bible story have you enjoyed the most?"

Into the Bible

"That's easy," James said, spreading his arms like giant wings. "The story of the seven-headed, gigantic red dragon trying to get the Baby, heaven, the woman, and then us! That story was intense!"

"Yes, I remember you talking about that story last night," Dad said. Then turning to Paul, he said, "May I have a look at this special Bible?"

"Sure!" Paul said excitedly. "I'll go get it." Paul ran to his room and came back with *The Prophet Kids' Bible*. "Here it is, Dad."

Dad opened it to the book of Revelation and flipped through until he found chapter 12. "Here's the story you were just talking about," Dad said, looking at James.

"Yeah, we read the whole thing when we got back," James said. "It's an awesome story. Everything is so powerful in Revelation."

Dad looked up. "You just reminded me of a really cool quote I read about the book of Revelation," he said. "It said that Revelation was not about the love of power, but about the power of love."

"That is cool," Paul said.

"Hey, what's this?" Dad asked, pointing at the open Bible. "One of the words, in the middle of Revelation twelve, is a different color." His finger was getting closer as he talked. The kids all got as close as they could, trying to see what Dad had found. Dad leaned forward, his finger right above the page. "It's red!" He moved his finger as if he were going to tap the red word.

James grabbed Dad's hand and yanked it away from the Bible. "Don't touch it!" he nearly shouted. "Haven't you been listening? You'll get sucked in!"

Dad started to laugh. "You guys are too much!" He looked down at the page. "It's the word *kingdom*," Dad said. "Does that mean all the stories in your next study will be about kingdoms?"

"Yes," Paul said. "It sure does!"

Thought Questions: Chapter 1
1. What is your favorite way to use your imagination?
2. How is your imagination used when you read the Bible?
3. What do you think *The Kingdom Scroll* is going to be about?

Chapter 2
The Great Controversy

James and Hannah crowded around the Bible with Dad and Paul.

"There it is," Paul said. "The next red word."

"What's it doing in the back?" James asked. "Both of the other two red words were in Genesis, at the beginning of the Bible."

"Maybe because we have been here before," Hannah said.

"Yeah, but I don't remember this section," James said. "It's right in the middle of the dragon story. But I don't remember hearing or seeing it."

"It's weird that we explored this story in the serpent scroll and didn't hear this part," Paul said.

"Look around the word *kingdom*. It's part of a huge poem or something," James said. "It says that a loud voice shouted across the heavens. And the word *kingdom* is in the first part of what the voice shouted."

Paul read aloud, " 'It has come at last—salvation and power and the Kingdom of our God, and the authority of his Christ.' That's the middle section of Revelation twelve, verse ten. And then there is a bunch more that the voice shouted."

"So," Dad interjected, "this part wasn't in the dragon story you explored yesterday?"

"Nope," James said. "It was just all the action scenes."

"That's it!" Paul said, excitedly slapping his hand to the table.

"What?" Hannah and James said together.

"We were exploring only the action and focusing closely on the dragon," Paul said. "And now, we are supposed to go back into the dragon scene to see what it shows us about God's kingdom."

"The starting point is here because we've been here before," James recapped, "and we need to have the dragon story as background to understand the kingdom story."

"That sounds about right," Paul said.

"Makes sense," Hannah said.

"Does it?" Dad asked. He looked very confused. He had been darting his eyes from one person to the next as they had been talking so far. "How does it make sense?"

"Without the dragon story," Paul explained, "the kingdom story wouldn't make sense."

"Or at least," James added, "it would be hard to figure out."

"I see," Dad said. "I think."

"In other words," Hannah said, "we need to review the dragon story before we put our fingers on the word *kingdom* and go spiraling into the Bible again."

Dad was starting to get it. "So," he said, "you need to understand the great controversy and its impact on the state of the world before you can really explore the meaning of the kingdom of God?"

The conversation came to a grinding halt. All three kids looked at Dad.

"What?" James asked as only James could—with his whole body.

"The great, what?" Hannah added.

"The great controversy," Dad said, "the war between God and Satan that started in heaven and moved to earth when Adam and Eve sinned. Satan equals sin. Jesus equals salvation. That whole epic story is called the great controversy."

"Cool," James said. "Makes it sound really important!"

Dad laughed. "It is really important! Revelation twelve—the dragon story—is the entire story of the Bible in one prophecy. It is epic."

The Great Controversy

"Sounds like a movie," Paul said.

James cut in, "Yeah, 'The Epic: Great Controversy!' You've read the book, now see the movie!"

"That's not bad, James," Dad said. "You may have a future in advertising."

Hannah pulled them back to the topic. "Dad, how does this great controversy help us understand the word *kingdom*?"

"Well"—Dad looked down at the Bible and skimmed the twelfth chapter of Revelation—"right after the dragon is kicked out of heaven and lands on the earth, it says the kingdom of God and the authority of Christ begin."

"Before the dragon chases the woman in the desert?" Paul asked, leaning over to look at the passage. "That means we are already living in the kingdom it is talking about."

"We are already in heaven?" Hannah asked.

"I don't think so!" James said, waving his arms around. "This world is nothing like heaven!"

"It must be talking about something else," Paul said. "What do you think, Dad?"

Dad folded his arms and leaned back in his chair, a huge smile growing on his face. "I think you three have another Bible adventure to go on!"

"Yeah," James jumped up, "let's take the Bible back to the room and go in!"

"Wait," Paul said, studying Dad's face. "You know something. Tell us!"

Dad's smile got even bigger. "I know that I want to hear your story when you get back! So, get into the Bible!"

Hannah joined the fight now, "Dad, come on! If you know something, you have to tell us!"

"Do I?" Dad laughed. "I know what some of your Christmas presents are. Should I tell you that?"

"There are already Christmas presents in the house?" James asked incredulously.

The Kingdom Scroll

"I didn't say that," Dad explained. "I said, I know what they are. They could still be in the store, or they could be here. But that's not the point. Christmas would be ruined if I told you all your presents."

"Ah," Paul said, finally understanding. "So, you're saying if you told us what you know, it would ruin our kingdom Bible adventure."

"Uh-huh," Dad said confidently. "Some things are best discovered on the journey rather than beforehand."

"OK," James said, still standing. "Let's go!"

Paul threw his hands up like a blockade. "First, let's say what we know."

"Yeah," Hannah said. "Let's make sure we are ready."

"Fine," James said, expelling all the air in his lungs with exasperation. "We know there's a kingdom in the dragon story."

"More than that," Paul added, "we know the kingdom is around before the woman runs into the desert."

"When was that?" Hannah asked. "I mean in history."

Paul looked at Dad, "Can you tell us that?"

"Think about it," Dad answered.

"Oh," James spun in a little circle, "I know! Satan was kicked out of heaven right before he went into the Garden of Eden. So, it must be back then."

Dad nodded. "There have been kingdoms all the way through the Bible. That's all I'm going to say!"

"I guess we just need to get going," Paul said. "We'll figure out each kingdom when we get to it."

"Yes!" James shouted as he grabbed for the Bible.

Paul snatched it first. "I will bring the Bible," he said. "You are dangerous!"

"Yeah," Hannah said, "you wouldn't want to put another hole in it!"

James put his hands on his hips, "Hey, Paul forgave me for that. Now you're supposed to forget about it! You know, forgive and forget!"

"Oh no," Paul said, carefully picking up the Bible as he rose to his

The Great Controversy

feet, "I'm not forgetting anything that puts this awesome Bible at risk!"

"Fair enough," James said as the three kids walked out of the living room.

"You kids have fun in the Bible," Dad said from the table.

"We will!" came the reply in three separate voices.

Thought Questions: Chapter 2
1. What is the great controversy? How would you explain it to a friend?
2. Dad seems to know something. What do you think he might know?
3. How many kingdoms can you name from the Bible?

Chapter 3
A Loud Speech

The three kids now stood at Paul's desk, *The Prophet Kids' Bible* open in front of them. Paul picked up the four scroll cards that were lying on the desk where he had left them earlier. On the back of each card were the words *scroll card* and a background picture that looked just like the cover of Paul's Bible. He turned the cards over and placed them face up in a row on the desk above the Bible.

Two of the cards had writing on their faces. One had the title "The Serpent Scroll" and under it were a list of Bible stories exploring the topic of serpents. The next card had the title "The Lamb Scroll," with stories listed underneath all referring to lambs. To the right of the list of stories on the second card were little pictures representing what the kids had learned in each story.

"When we touch the red word," Paul said, "one of the last two scroll cards will be activated."

"And the title will appear!" Hannah said.

"And we will be pulled into the Bible," James added.

"That's right," Paul said. "So, should we touch the red *kingdom* in Revelation chapter twelve, verse four, and start the adventure?"

"Yeah!" James said, thrusting his hand toward the page.

"Wait," Hannah pushed James's hand down so it missed the desk

A Loud Speech

and ended up back at his side. "I want to know what the words in the Bible say before we go in."

"Of course, you would," James grumbled. "You always want to know everything!"

"I just don't want to get caught by surprise, like in the first adventure," Hannah said. "And I don't want to get stuck in the Bible, like we did in the second adventure!"

"We figured them both out," James said. "And we made it back home safely!"

Hannah crossed her arms across her chest. "Just read what it says in this story."

James threw his hands up in defeat. "Fine," he said. "Read the dragon story—*again*!" He stressed the word *again* as if it were the worst thing in the world.

"Well," Paul said, scanning the text, "you remember the dragon flew to heaven and back, trying to conquer everything."

"Yes," Hannah said.

"This is a speech in the middle of the story." Paul picked up the Bible and read aloud:

> Then I heard a loud voice shouting across the heavens,
>
> > "It has come at last—
> > > salvation and power
> > and the Kingdom of our God,
> > > and the authority of his Christ."

"There's the word *kingdom* that we're going to follow," Hannah interjected.

"Yes," Paul said. "Keep listening, there's more in the speech."

> > "For the accuser of our brothers and sisters
> > > has been thrown down to earth—

> the one who accuses them
> > before our God day and night."

"That's Satan!" James cut in. "He is always telling lies about us and trying to make us look bad!"

"True," Paul replied. "There is still half of the speech to go. Keep listening."

> "And they have defeated him by the blood of the Lamb
> > and by their testimony."

"Hey!" Hannah clapped her hands together, "That's Jesus, the perfect Lamb, from the Lamb scroll!"

"That's right!" James added. "Is there any more to the speech?"

"Yes," Paul said. "I know you two are excited, but just let me finish reading it!" Hannah and James looked at each other, smiled, and nodded. They were very excited about this new adventure. Paul continued reading.

> "And they did not love their lives so much
> > that they were afraid to die.
> Therefore, rejoice, O heavens!
> > And you who live in the heavens, rejoice!
> But terror will come on the earth and the sea,
> > for the devil has come down to you in great anger,
> > > knowing that he has little time."

"That's the end of the speech," Paul said. "Clearly, that's the moment when the dragon landed back on earth after being kicked out of heaven."

"Yeah," James looked at the speech as Paul laid the Bible back on the desk. "All the terrible things happening around the earth making people sick, angry, and evil are because of that last part." James pointed at one phrase in the speech and tapped each word as he finished his sentence,

A Loud Speech

"The devil is 'in great anger' because he's almost out of time."

"Because Jesus is coming back soon," Hannah said. "Right?"

"Right," Paul answered. "Satan is doing everything he can to make life on earth as bad as possible so God's people will be hurt and reject God because they think He doesn't love them."

"That's what we learned in the serpent scroll," Hannah remembered.

"Yeah, that's right," James was leaning over the open Bible, reading the speech again to himself. He was mumbling the words quietly as he read. "Well," he said after a few seconds of reading, "I think we've got a grip on what's going on in the story. Let's get into it!"

"Explain it to me," Hannah said.

"Are you for real?" James spun around and looked at his little sister. "What do you not understand?"

"I just don't get why God's kingdom is at the top of the speech before Satan is attacking earth and all the people on it," Hannah replied. "Shouldn't God's kingdom be after Jesus comes back and takes us away from all this bad stuff?"

James looked up at Paul, "Go for it, bro!"

Paul smiled and said, "Well, Hannah, perhaps we will be able to answer that question once we've gone into the Bible." He placed his hand on his little sister's shoulder. "I don't think there is anything to be afraid of. We've already been through the dragon story. Let's just go for it!"

"Now you're talking!" James said, slapping Paul on the back. "Let's do it." James moved his finger toward the red word for the second time. Hannah and Paul joined him. Three little fingers approached the center of the open Bible and rested on the word *kingdom*.

Nothing happened. Or at least they thought nothing had happened.

Thought Questions: Chapter 3

1. Why does Hannah want to know more before entering the Bible?
2. How is Satan like a dragon? How is Jesus like a lamb?
3. Describe God's kingdom. What would it be like to live in it?

Chapter 4
A Kingdom Dream

"What?" James exclaimed. "It didn't work!"

"That is weird," Hannah said. "We didn't do anything wrong. That's what we've always done, and we've always gone zipping into the middle of a blank white page."

"Hey," Paul said. "Look at that!" He reached forward and picked up one of the two remaining scroll cards. Now emblazoned across the top of the card were the words *The Kingdom Scroll* and underneath were the words for the first story. James and Hannah leaned in and studied the card with Paul.

"How can the first story be there already?" Hannah asked. "We haven't even been in the Bible yet!"

"A Kingdom Dream," Paul read the story title out loud. "What story could that be?"

"How can a kingdom dream?" Hannah asked. "A king could dream, but not a kingdom!"

"That's it!" James nearly jumped right out of his skin. "'A kingdom dream!' A king did dream that!"

"What are you talking about?" Paul asked, turning toward his brother and scrunching his eyebrows together. "Please explain."

"There's a story somewhere in the Bible," James said, "where a king

A Kingdom Dream

dreams about a bunch of kingdoms."

"Of course"—Paul slapped his own forehead—"why didn't I think of that? It's Nebuchadnezzar's dream of the big statue."

"Nebu—who?" Hannah asked, puzzled.

"King Nebuchadnezzar, the king of Babylon," Paul answered. "He dreamed of a statue made out of all different metals."

"Its head was gold," James said.

"That's right," Paul said. "And every section of the statue was a different kind of metal."

"Why did he dream that?" Hannah asked.

"Let's look it up," Paul said. "Then we can read the story before we go into it."

"Cool," James said. "Then we'll know everything that is supposed to happen and nothing will trap us!"

"What part of the Bible is it in?" Hannah asked.

Paul smiled. "I'll give you a hint. There was only one man who could explain the king's dream."

"Joseph!" Hannah shouted, jumping up and down on the spot.

Paul laughed at how excited Hannah was. "That's funny! You are correct that Joseph interpreted a dream for the king of Egypt. But this is a different story and a different king!"

"Wasn't it Daniel who explained the statue dream?" James asked.

"That's it!" Paul said, congratulating James. "Well done. So, what book of the Bible do you think it's in?"

"Uh," James said, tapping on his head in mock frustration. "Duh, maybe, uh—Daniel?"

Hannah and Paul laughed at their ever-entertaining brother.

"Right on, again," Paul said, flipping through the Bible until he came to the book of Daniel.

He started scanning the chapter titles and found it very quickly.

"Chapter two," Paul said, "Nebuchadnezzar's Dream is the chapter title."

The Kingdom Scroll

"Can you read it to us?" Hannah said. "Like you did with the speech?"

"I guess so," Paul answered, picking up the Bible and sitting on the chair. Facing his brother and sister, he began to read.

"One night during the second year of his reign, Nebuchadnezzar had such disturbing dreams that he couldn't sleep. He called in his magicians, enchanters, sorcerers, and astrologers, and he demanded that they tell him what he had dreamed."

As Paul continued reading aloud, both James and Hannah began imagining the scene being described.

The king became angrier and angrier as each supposed wise man was unable to tell him what he had dreamed. Each man begged the king to tell them the dream and they would tell him the meaning. "That's how it's always done," the men said to the king. "You tell us the dream and we tell you the meaning. No one can do what you are asking!"

Amazingly, Nebuchadnezzar became so angry that he decided to kill all his wise men. Then Daniel heard about the death sentence. He begged the king for more time, and time was given. He asked his friends to pray. Then he went to sleep. When he woke up, he had dreamed the same dream as the king! And he knew what it meant! He rushed to the king to tell him the good news.

As Daniel told the king the dream—a statue made of many kinds of metal—both James and Hannah imagined it with such vivid detail it was as if they were there. Then Daniel started to explain the dream, "But after your kingdom comes to an end, another kingdom, inferior to yours, will rise to take your place. After that kingdom . . ."

Each time they heard the word *kingdom*, the story got fuzzier in their imagination until, on the third *kingdom*, James said, "Hey, there's the word *kingdom*. Is it red?"

Hannah and James stood to look at the page where Paul had been reading.

Paul stopped and looked up from the Bible. "Do you want me to stop reading?"

A Kingdom Dream

"We just heard the word *kingdom* lots of times," Hannah said. "Is it red?"

"No," Paul said.

"How are we going to get into the Bible?" Hannah asked. "We need a red word to touch."

"The scroll card was already activated when we touched the red word in Revelation," Paul said. "My guess is that all we need to do is put our fingers on the scroll card, and it will take us into the story."

"Why didn't we go in before," James asked, "when we touched *kingdom* in the dragon story in Revelation?"

Hannah answered, "We already figured that out, James! We needed to look at the dragon story again so we could see how God's kingdom and Satan's kingdom have been fighting since Satan was kicked out of heaven."

"Oh yeah," James said. "That makes sense."

"Well," Paul said, "Do you want to touch it and see if we go into this story?"

James and Hannah looked at each other excitedly and then back at the Bible.

"It's a really good story," James said.

"I wanna hear the rest, right now!" Hannah said.

"I wanna see the rest!" James added.

"Let's touch the kingdom scroll card," Paul said, "and see what happens."

"*Woo-hoo!*" James pumped his fist in the air. "Here we go." Then with a mocking smile, he added, "Again."

"You don't think it will work this time?" Hannah asked.

"Let's find out," Paul said, holding the new scroll card in front of him. All three children reached toward the kingdom scroll card with pointed fingers. Their fingers touched the card in unison, and they felt the familiar pull of the Bible drawing them into yet another adventure.

The words on the kingdom scroll card began to ripple like waves in a

The Kingdom Scroll

pond after a stone is dropped onto its smooth surface. The three kids were being squished against each other and seemed to be shrinking—or the scroll card was growing. They felt themselves being pulled toward the card. They saw the word *kingdom* grow larger and larger until they went right through the *g* in the middle of the word.

As they popped through to the other side of the scroll card, they saw the Bible on Paul's desk. The words were rippling on its pages too. As they catapulted toward the Bible, the rippling effect changed to a spiral and the children felt themselves being pulled closer and closer to the Bible. The words on the pages blurred, leaving a blank expanse of white paper.

The three children landed with a *thud* inside the Bible again.

Thought Questions: Chapter 4

1. Do you like listening to someone read a book to you? Why?
2. What word distracted the kids from their imagining? Why?
3. Do you know the story of the statue in Nebuchadnezzar's dream? Tell it.

Chapter 5
A Palace Appearing

Paul, James, and Hannah stood facing each other, as they had been moments before, with the scroll card between them.

The boys' bedroom was gone. Everything was gone. They were surrounded by an unending and incomprehensible environment of white. White ground, white sky, even the air seemed to be white.

James took his finger off the scroll card and spun in a quick circle. He threw his arms into the air and jumped with glee, "Yes! It worked! We're in the Bible again!"

"We sure are," Paul said. "Now we just need to fill in the page."

"We have to guess the words on the page," James said, regaining control of his excitement.

Hannah shook her head. "We don't have to guess this time," she said confidently. "We know where we are. We were just reading the story!"

"Of course," James said. "We're in the second chapter of Daniel, where Nebuchadnezzar is having bad dreams!"

Just as James mentioned Nebuchadnezzar, a throne appeared a few paces in front of the children. And on the throne sat a man who looked very tired. A crown rested on the arm of the massive throne next to the man. His red, puffy eyes were staring right at the three kids.

The king leaned forward on his throne, clenched his fists, and shouted at the kids, "I can see through your trick! You are trying to stall for time because you know I am serious about what I said."

Hannah rushed behind her big brother Paul. James turned toward Paul with a look of anguish on his face. "Is he talking to us?"

The king, sitting on his throne that was still surrounded by white nothingness, continued his tirade: "If you don't tell me the dream, you will be condemned. You have conspired to tell me lies in hopes that something will change. But tell me the dream, and then I will know that you can tell me what it means."

"He is talking to us!" James said while breathing rapid fire. "What is happening?"

Paul whispered, "I don't know. We've always just seen the stories as invisible witnesses. But, if he is talking to us, I bet he can hear us!"

"Are you going to answer me?" The king bellowed. He looked like he was going to explode from his throne and rip them to shreds at any moment.

Hannah was shaking with fear behind her brother. She held tightly to his arm. "Do you really think, somehow, we have become the king's wise men?"

Less than a second after Hannah said, "Wise men," a shaky voice from behind the kids said, "There isn't a man alive who can tell Your Majesty his dream!"

All three children spun around and saw a group of finely dressed men cowering, lying on the white ground. One of the wise men was on his knees, with his hands clasped together. He was clearly the man who had just spoken.

"And no king, however great and powerful, has ever asked such a thing of any magician, enchanter, or astrologer!" The man crawled toward the children. They parted and let him pass. He covered about half of the distance between the children and the king before uttering his final line as a whisper, clearly begging for mercy, "This is an impossible thing the king requires. No one except the gods can tell you your dream,

A Palace Appearing

and they do not live among people."

King Nebuchadnezzar grasped the front of his armrests like a rower pulling on his oars. He was rocking forward and backward in rage. "You will all die!" he shouted. "Guards!" From the white expanse to the left and right of the throne, two guards materialized. "Take these men to the gallows. They are to be killed for their insolence!"

The guards stamped their feet and saluted. They gathered up the quivering men and dragged them into the distant whiteness.

The king's rage was building in both volume and action. He rose to his feet and shouted, "Arioch!" A tall soldier walked quickly past the children, "Yes, my king?"

With a sweeping gesture, Nebuchadnezzar commanded, "Find all of my wise men—every last one of them—and slaughter them all! They are a worthless lot. They lie. They have no power. They only make up answers to please me, not to reveal the truth. Kill them all!"

Arioch, the commander of the king's guard, stamped his feet and saluted. "It will be done," he said and then turned and left the room.

The king slumped back into his throne. He sat, shaking and alone.

Hannah stepped out from behind Paul. She turned from side to side, exploring the world around them. Or, more precisely, the lack of a world around them. "Why is everything still white?" she wondered aloud. "Every other story we've explored has been in full color, as if we were really there. But this time, only the people are in color."

"And the throne," James said. He had been wondering the same thing. "Why hasn't the rest of Babylon appeared?"

Instantly, a world of color, beauty, and wealth surrounded the three siblings. They stood in a mighty palace. The king on his throne, which, just moments before, had seemed so large, was now dwarfed by the room in which he sat. The floor and massive pillars were made of shiny marble. The roof was laced with golden lines and patterns. And the walls were covered with thick tapestries that looked as if they came from every corner of the world.

The Kingdom Scroll

The children spun in circles trying to take it all in. Hannah began to giggle. Then James joined in. Finally, Paul smiled and said, "We forgot to say where we were!"

"We knew," Hannah said. "Because we had been reading the story. But, when we got here, the story didn't know us!"

"It knows us now," James said, with a laugh.

"It certainly appears that way," Paul said, with an intelligent glint in his eye. "Get it?"

"A joke?" James clasped his hands to the sides of his head. "Paul made a joke?"

"It certainly *appears* that way," Paul said again, his face spreading into a big grin.

Hannah giggled again. "You're right! It did appear that way! That's a good one, Paul."

"We say it," Paul said, "And . . ." He paused to let his siblings finish the sentence.

"It appears!"

Thought Questions: Chapter 5
1. Why did the kids think the king was talking to them?
2. Why was the king so upset? Do you think the wise men will all die?
3. Why did it take so long for the entire scene to appear for the kids?

Bible Adventurer Bonus:

You can read this story in Daniel 2.

Chapter 6
With All Respect

As the children explored every nook and cranny of the palace courtroom, the king sat sullenly on his throne. Occasionally he would clear his throat and sit forward as if he were about to say something. Then, looking around the empty room, he would slump back into his huge throne. His eyes were bloodshot from a lack of sleep. His hands fidgeted restlessly, moving from the armrests to his lap, then rubbing his eyes and smoothing his hair. He was obviously distressed about his dream.

After ten or fifteen minutes, Arioch rushed back into the room and bowed some distance from where the king sat on his throne. "Permission to speak, my king?"

The king sat straighter in his throne and beckoned for Arioch to approach. The three children, distracted from their exploring by the arrival of Arioch, followed the soldier to the throne. They wanted to hear Arioch's message.

Arioch stopped a few steps in front of the king's throne. "I'm sorry to bother you with this, my king, but I think you will want to hear this."

"Go ahead," the king said.

The three kids stood next to Arioch.

"As I was rounding up the magicians, enchanters, and astrologers, one of them asked to see you," Arioch said.

The Kingdom Scroll

"Wants to beg for his life, does he?" The king said with a sneer.

"Yes, sir," Arioch said, "and he thinks he may be able to explain your dream."

"Sure, sure," the king said, not believing. "We shall see. Send him in."

Arioch stamped his feet and saluted before turning to walk quickly from the room.

Hannah turned to the boys, "Is this when Daniel comes in?"

"I think so," Paul answered.

James started walking toward the throne. "Come on, guys; they can't see us. Let's go stand next to the king so we can see and hear everything really well."

"Good idea," Paul said. He and Hannah followed James until they were all standing next to King Nebuchadnezzar. None of them had gotten this close to him while exploring the room.

"It's so weird," Hannah said.

"What is?" James asked.

"Being able to see people when they can't see or hear us," Hannah answered. "I know we are inside the Bible, not in the real place, but it's still scary. I'm always afraid someone is going to look at us and say, 'Are you kids about finished? Get out of here!' It's just so real!"

James leaned over the armrest of the throne and put his face about three inches from King Nebuchadnezzar's face. "It's like a three-dimensional movie that you can walk right into," he said, blowing on the king's cheek.

"Stop it," Paul said. "You're being disrespectful!"

"Disrespectful of what?" James shot back. "To him, we're not here. It's just a story, and we are reading it from the inside rather than the outside of the book."

"Yes," Paul said, "I know that. But you are still acting disrespectful. Enjoy the story with respect for the characters."

"Just like when we read the Bible," Hannah said, pulling James away from the throne. "You wouldn't make faces while someone was reading it to you. Or you wouldn't call the stories dumb or laugh at them."

"That's true, Hannah," Paul said. "The Bible is God's Holy Book. We should treat it with respect all the time."

"OK, OK," James huffed. "I get it. I'll be respectful from now on. It's just cool that we can get right in their faces, and they don't even know it."

"It's not cool," Paul said. "The way you treat others, especially when they can't see you, says more about you than it does about them."

James's shoulders slumped forward. He knew Paul and Hannah were right. He liked having fun, but sometimes that fun caused him to do or say things that hurt other people's feelings. "I'll try to be more respectful," he said in a whisper.

Hannah and Paul hugged their brother. They knew he meant it.

Just then Arioch came back into the room with a finely dressed man following him. The two men stopped in the middle of the room.

"My king," Arioch said in a loud formal voice, "I present to you one of your wise men, Belteshazzar."

Hannah turned to look at her brothers. "I thought it would be Daniel. Who is this?"

"He is Daniel," Paul whispered. "Belteshazzar is the name they gave him when he was captured and trained as a Babylonian wise man."

"Why are you whispering?" James said loudly. "They can't hear you!"

"Respect!" Both Hannah and Paul said at once.

James eyes opened wide in embarrassment, and he threw his hand across his mouth. "Sorry," he whispered from behind his hand. "I forgot!"

"Already?" Paul asked, shaking his head in mock amazement. Then he smiled and patted James on the back. "You'll get it, sooner or later."

James dropped his hand to his side and smiled.

"You may come," King Nebuchadnezzar said, beckoning toward Daniel.

Daniel took three steps forward and then bowed his head low. He took another three steps and again bowed his head. After a few more triple steps and head bows, he arrived at the throne and dropped to his knees, pressing his forehead to the ground, his hands lying on the floor in front of his head. He waited like that.

"Belteshazzar, you may rise," the king said. "And you may speak."

Daniel slowly rose to his knees and faced the king, keeping his head lower than Nebuchadnezzar's. "My king, I kneel before you, begging for time."

"Time?" The king asked. "I thought you would be begging for your life. What use is time? A few extra hours before your death will only be spent agonizing about the inevitable! You will die with the rest of the useless soothsayers." The king spat the last word as if it were a mouthful of dirt.

"If I were given time to pray and to sleep," Daniel lifted his eyes to meet the king's gaze, "I believe my God might reveal your dream and its meaning to me as I sleep."

"Oh, really?" The king leaned forward in his chair. "You're not just trying to get an extra night's sleep before you go to the gallows?"

"How could I sleep," Daniel said, "if I knew I would die when I woke? I need to sleep in peace, knowing my king and my God both show mercy to me."

"Very well," Nebuchadnezzar said, leaning back into his throne. "One night. And tomorrow, I tell Arioch to begin killing men unless I hear both my dream and its meaning!"

Daniel bowed again, pressing his forehead to the ground.

"See that," Paul whispered, pointing at Daniel. "That is respect."

"I'll say," James agreed. "It almost looks like he's worshiping the king."

"No, he's not," Paul said. "He just knows his place in front of the king."

Hannah turned to join the conversation, "Twice he told the king he would be relying on his God to reveal the dream. The king clearly knows that Daniel worships God."

"Good point," Paul said.

With All Respect

Daniel rose to his knees and spoke, "Thank you, my king. You are most gracious." Then Daniel stood, turned slowly, and walked toward the exit.

"Let's follow him," Hannah said excitedly.

"Yeah," James said, rubbing his hands together. "I bet we will get to see Shadrach, Meshach, and Abednego!"

"Cool," Paul said. "Let's go."

The three children ran to catch up with Daniel and followed him out of the palace of King Nebuchadnezzar and into the world of ancient Babylon.

Thought Questions: Chapter 6
1. What was disrespectful about James's actions?
2. Why is it important to be respectful to others, even when they are not present?
3. What is the difference between showing respect and worshiping?

Bible Adventurer Bonus:

You can read this story in Daniel 2.

Chapter 7
Following Daniel

As the children walked out of the throne room, they entered a colonnade; beautiful flowers growing from vines wrapped around the massive marble columns. Everywhere they looked there was beauty and life.

"It's so beautiful," Hannah said, trying to look in every direction at once so she wouldn't miss anything.

"It sure is," James said, as they walked out of the palace and onto a large terrace. James ran to a low wall on the edge of the terrace and stared in wonder at what he saw. "Guys," he shouted to the others, "come look at this!"

Hannah and Paul forced their attention away from all the wonders their eyes were exploring, and walked over to where James stood.

"Look what I found," James said as if he were an archaeologist who had just discovered a lost pharaoh's tomb.

The other two leaned over the marble wall and struggled to make sense of what they were seeing. James joined them, peering into the courtyard below them.

"That's a lot of plants," Hannah said in wonder.

"But they are at all different heights," James added.

Below the children was a massive garden filled with all kinds of exotic trees, flowers, plants, and flowing water.

Following Daniel

"How is that even possible?" James asked. "It's like the Garden of Eden inside of a man-made courtyard."

"It's the Hanging Gardens of Babylon," Paul said in awe. "King Nebuchadnezzar had them built for his wife."

"As a wedding present?" Hannah asked in amazement.

"No," Paul said. "She was homesick for Persia. So, he brought the beauty of Persian trees and plants to Babylon. It's one of the seven wonders of the ancient world."

"That is so cool," James said. "What a dude! Looking after his lady."

"It's so romantic," Hannah said. Then turning around, she blurted, "Oh, no! Daniel is gone!"

The boys spun around and searched the terrace. They had become so distracted by the beauty of the gardens that they forgot to stay with Daniel.

"We gotta run and catch him," James said.

"He could be anywhere by now," Paul answered. "We better just stay here, or we will get lost in this massive city. Let's just explore the palace and the gardens until Daniel returns."

"That's going to be a long time!" Hannah said. "He's going home to pray and have a sleep."

"*Hmm,*" Paul said. "You're right. He won't be back until tomorrow morning."

Even though each of the three kids was now facing in different directions, they all saw what happened next. Hannah, who was peering into the gardens, saw the plants begin to flash on and off. James, who was looking across the huge terrace, saw the marble slabs flipping from their natural white color to black. Paul, who was studying the sky, watched in wonder as it carved itself into multiple tiles that began spinning, alternating between blue and inky black. Soon, the three children stood in utter darkness.

"Uh, guys," James said. "What's going on?"

"I think we are transitioning to a new scene," Paul said. "Into another part of the story."

"So, we have to guess where we are?" Hannah asked.

"I don't think so," James said in a distracted voice. "I can kinda see something."

"You can?" both Paul and Hannah said together.

"Yeah," James answered. "I think my eyes are just getting used to the dark."

Paul looked around, trying to see. "You're right! I can see the terrace reflecting the moonlight. But it is very faint."

Hannah clapped her hands, "Yes, I can see too. We're still in the same place. I can feel the wall we were leaning on, and I can barely see some of the trees in the garden below us."

"So," James said, thinking aloud, "we haven't gone anywhere!"

Just then they heard footsteps in the darkness. There were a few people walking together from the sound. When they got closer, the kids could make out whispering voices.

"You really saw the dream?" one voice said.

"And its meaning?" another added.

"Yes!" a third voice answered. "We must find Arioch."

"That's Daniel!" James said, jumping toward the voices. "Let's follow them!"

"Yes!" Paul said excitedly. "It must be the next morning. Come on, Hannah!" Paul grabbed his sister's hand, and they hurried after James, following the voices in the dark.

Soon they were right behind the group of men. There were four of them. They walked briskly across the terrace and into another wing of the palace. There were lots of doors to the right and left.

"Which one is Arioch's room?" one voice asked.

"The one on the very end," Daniel answered. "The corner room. It has the best view of the city streets. Arioch is always looking for ways to keep his finger on the pulse of Babylon."

Suddenly, the men stopped walking. "This is it," Daniel said, as he raised his hand and knocked firmly three times.

Following Daniel

A scuffling noise came toward the door. A bar was lifted from the other side and the door swung into the room. Arioch stepped out, fully dressed, holding a torch that blazed into the darkness. "Yes?"

"I have seen the king's dream," Daniel said quickly.

"And also the meaning?" Arioch asked seriously, his expression revealed by the torchlight.

Daniel and the three men with him all answered together, "Yes!"

"Come with me," Arioch said, taking Daniel by the arm. Then pushing the torch toward the other men, he examined their faces. "You three, go home. No need for a fan club."

"Yes, sir," the others said together.

Daniel and Arioch headed back down the corridor, the light of the torch leading the way. The other men and the three children followed behind at a respectable distance until Paul said, "Come on, guys. We don't want to let Daniel get away again."

They ran to catch up with Daniel and Arioch, leaving Daniel's three friends behind. They had to run just to match the pace Arioch was setting. He was a big man—and he was in a hurry.

"I do not wish to kill our own men," Arioch said, as they walked. "I truly hope you are telling the truth."

"God is most gracious," Daniel replied.

They rounded a corner and stepped into the large courtroom of the king. Arioch let go of Daniel's arm. "You stay here. I will go see if the king has arisen from his bed. It is very early, but the king has not been sleeping well since his troubling dream." Arioch walked into the distance, the light of his torch becoming smaller and fainter as he went.

"Dear God," Daniel's whisper startled the children, "You have given me the dream and its meaning. Now please bless me with the right words to say before the king. Amen."

"Amen," the three kids said together before smiling at each other in the darkness.

Thought Questions: Chapter 7

1. Why do you think Arioch didn't want to kill the wise men?
2. List some attributes of Daniel's and Arioch's characters that made them good servants.
3. Why did Daniel pray before talking to the king?

Chapter 8

A Dream Revealed

After what seemed like an eternity, three lights emerged from a corridor at the other end of the large room. Although it was a long way away, it was good to have some light in the oppressive darkness.

Daniel, who had been standing perfectly still the entire time, now moved his weight from one foot to the other and made rustling noises as he ran his hands over his robes to remove any wrinkles.

The three lights moved across the room and stopped in line with Daniel and the kids but still at the far end of the room. The flickering torches paused there for a few minutes and then one of the lights started to grow brighter and larger. The sound of footsteps came into earshot, and then, moments later, the muscled bulk of Arioch appeared as he approached Daniel.

"You may come," Arioch said. "The king is anxious to hear what you have to say." The hand that was not holding the torch reached out and rested on Daniel's shoulder, guiding him. The two men headed across the room.

The three kids fell in behind the two men and followed closely enough to the light to see where they were stepping.

"I think we are in the throne room," James whispered.

"Yes," Paul agreed. "The other two lights must be guards standing on

The Kingdom Scroll

either side of Nebuchadnezzar and his throne."

The children continued following Arioch and Daniel in silence for a while and then Hannah noticed something. "Hey, guys," she said, "I think I can see morning light. Look left or right and then scan your eyes slowly up from the floor."

"Oh, yes! I see it," James said. "There are long slits of light along the top of where the walls must end."

"I think it's an overhanging roof," Paul said, "so the light can come in, but the rain can't."

"It must be morning," Hannah said, as she continued walking with her brothers.

"That will be nice," James said. "I'm a little tired of being in the dark!"

Arioch stomped his feet twice and stopped walking. Daniel stopped beside him, standing in silence.

Before Arioch could announce Daniel to the king, an anxious voice came from the throne, "Belteshazzar, Arioch tells me you know my dream! Is this true? Can you tell me what my dream was and what it means?"

Paul, James, and Hannah walked up next to Daniel so they could see the king. In the light of the torches, they could see deep lines on the king's face, and his eyes looked puffy and red.

"He looks very tired," James whispered.

"And like he's been crying," Hannah added.

"He is very distressed about this dream," Paul explained. "Distressed enough to threaten the lives of all his wisest advisers and religious leaders!"

Daniel replied, "There are no wise men, enchanters, magicians, or fortune-tellers who can tell the king such things."

The king thrust himself forward on his throne until he was on the very edge of his seat. His eyes were bulging in anger.

"Why would Daniel say that?" Hannah asked. "He knows the dream!"

"And its meaning," James said.

"He's a smart man," Paul said with quiet respect.

A Dream Revealed

"Smart?" James hissed in rebuke. "He's gonna get himself killed!"

After a pause, Daniel continued, "But there is a God in heaven who reveals secrets, and He has shown King Nebuchadnezzar what will happen in the future. Now I will tell you your dream and the visions you saw as you lay on your bed."

James clapped his hands once in amazement and then caught himself. "Sorry, guys," he said. "I'm trying to be respectful, but that was a great line. He's making the king want the answer even more."

"And," Paul said, "he gave credit to God for the dream that they both had."

"Daniel really loves God," Hannah said quietly. "Doesn't he?"

"Yeah," Paul said. "He wants all the glory to go to God, not to himself."

Daniel continued, "While Your Majesty was sleeping, you dreamed about coming events. The Revealer of mysteries has shown you what is going to happen. And it is not because I am wiser than any living person that I know the secret of your dream, but because God wanted you to understand what you were thinking about."

"You were right, Paul," Hannah said. "He's giving all the credit to God."

Daniel stepped forward and began talking in the singsong voice of a storyteller, "Your Majesty, in your vision you saw in front of you a huge and powerful statue of a man, shining brilliantly, frightening and awesome. The head of the statue was made of fine gold, its chest and arms were of silver, its belly and thighs were of bronze, its legs were of iron, and its feet were a combination of iron and clay."

The king nearly fell off his chair with excitement. "*Yes!*" He stood, started to walk forward, then, remembering who he was, sat down on the throne, scooted his weight to the back, and clasped the armrests. "Go on!" he nearly shouted.

Daniel smiled and continued, "As you watched, a rock was cut from a mountain without any human help. It struck the feet of iron and clay,

45

smashing them to bits. The entire statue collapsed into a heap of iron, clay, bronze, silver, and gold. The pieces were crushed as small as chaff on a threshing floor, and the wind blew them all away without a trace. But the rock that knocked the statue down became a great mountain that covered the entire earth."

The king clasped his hands together, squeezing them tightly. "That is my dream exactly!"

A rush of air burst from Arioch's lungs and forced its way through his pursed lips. He was clearly relieved that he wouldn't be required to kill anyone that day.

Leaning forward on his throne, the king said, "And the meaning! Do you truly know the meaning?" He sat back and rubbed his hands together in anticipation.

Daniel nodded and took another step toward the king, preparing to answer. Just then the morning sun hit the roof of the palace and light poured in through the slits at the top of the walls. The details of every person in the room were now clearly visible. Two burly guards stood stone-faced next to the throne, each holding a torch. Arioch stood with his legs wide apart, still holding a torch in one hand. And the king's puffy face had a smile of excitement as he stared intensely at Daniel.

Thought Questions: Chapter 8

1. Why did the dream bother the king so much?
2. Why does Daniel talk about God all the time? Why is this important?
3. Do you think the king will be happy with Daniel's interpretation of the dream? Why?

Bible Adventurer Bonus:

You can read this story in Daniel 2.

Chapter 9

Kingdom After Kingdom

Now standing in a fully lit room, Daniel began to explain the meaning of King Nebuchadnezzar's dream. "Your Majesty, you are a king over many kings. The God of heaven has given you sovereignty, power, strength, and honor. He has made you the ruler over all the inhabited world and has put even the animals and birds under your control. You are the head of gold."

The king nodded, welcoming the idea. "Of course, I am!" he said with pride. "I am the head of the entire world. Indeed the gods—all the gods—shine their light on me!"

Daniel paused to allow the king's interruption and then continued quickly, "But after your kingdom comes to an end, another great kingdom, inferior to yours, will rise to take your place."

Nebuchadnezzar shot to the front of his throne, again sitting at the edge of his seat. His face was turning red in anger.

Daniel rushed on, "After that kingdom has fallen, yet a third great kingdom, represented by the bronze belly and thighs, will rise to rule the world. Following that kingdom, there will be a fourth great kingdom, as strong as iron. That kingdom will smash and crush all previous empires, just as iron smashes and crushes everything it strikes."

The king slumped back into his chair. The enormous timeline of the dream was overwhelming him. Kingdoms reigned for hundreds of years. This dream was laying out the future for thousands of years. The ages to come were unraveling before him. Was it possible that he was only a small fish in the huge sea of time?

Daniel's explanation continued, "The feet and toes you saw that were a combination of iron and clay show that this kingdom will be divided. Some parts of it will be as strong as iron, and others as weak as clay. This mixture of iron and clay also shows that these kingdoms will try to strengthen themselves by forming alliances with each other through intermarriage. But this will not succeed, just as iron and clay do not mix."

"Iron and clay don't mix?" James asked.

"Evidently not," Paul murmured.

All three of the kids were as caught up in the story as the king was.

Daniel continued, "During the reigns of those kings, the God of heaven will set up a kingdom that will never be destroyed; no one will ever conquer it. It will shatter all these kingdoms into nothingness, but it will stand forever. That is the meaning of the rock cut from the mountain by supernatural means, crushing to dust the statue of iron, bronze, clay, silver, and gold."

"That's God's kingdom, isn't it?" Hannah asked.

"Yup," James said, throwing his head backward and forward in a huge nod.

"God's kingdom will never end," Paul said.

Daniel finished his interpretation, saying, "The great God has shown Your Majesty what will happen in the future. The dream is true, and its meaning is certain."

The king, who had been through so much emotional turmoil over the past few days and nights, raised his hands to his face, and rubbed his cheeks and eyes. His hands worked their way to the top of his head where the fingers laced together. He sat in silence, holding his head, staring at Daniel. It was impossible to read his face. There were so many feelings coursing through the king's heart and mind.

Kingdom After Kingdom

Slowly, the king lowered his hands to the armrests, and he pulled himself forward on the throne and stood up. He took a few steps away from his throne until he was a couple of paces from Daniel. Then, with great respect, King Nebuchadnezzar lowered himself to his knees. He stared up into the eyes of Daniel.

Daniel was clearly uncomfortable. He had never before had his head higher than the king's. Such insolence was punishable by death. But the king had knelt before him.

Next, the king pressed his hands and forehead to the marble floor in front of Daniel. Assuming he had passed out from his recent stress, all three soldiers hurried toward the king.

One of the king's hands lifted, ever so slightly, from the ground, a finger pointing in warning. Arioch stopped in his tracks and waved at the other two soldiers to stop. The king hadn't fainted. He was doing the unthinkable. He was worshiping Daniel.

"But he's a—" one of the guards blurted but stopped instantly as Arioch's huge hand grabbed the hilt of his sword. His angry glare was impossible to misunderstand. It clearly said, *You speak a word against the king and I'll kill you!*

"He's a what?" James said with frustration.

"A slave," Hannah whispered.

"And he's not Babylonian," Paul said. "Daniel clearly doesn't believe in the same god as Nebuchadnezzar does, and yet the king is worshiping him."

The king raised himself onto his knees and spoke, "Bring sweet incense to burn before this man, the wisest of all my counselors."

The guard who had just spoken in haste, now rushed behind the throne and brought out a small incense urn and lit it with a drop of burning oil from his torch. He laid the smoking pot at Daniel's feet and bowed once before returning to the king's side.

"Today shall be a day of sacrifice," the king said. Then looking up at Daniel, he said, "Belteshazzar, truly your God is the God of gods, the

The Kingdom Scroll

Lord over kings, a Revealer of mysteries, for you have been able to reveal this secret. We shall sacrifice to the God who knows all and speaks through His servant Belteshazzar."

"From now on," the king said, moving his gaze from Daniel to Arioch, "this man is to be my chief counselor. I want him within reach at all times."

Arioch nodded in agreement. Then the king returned his gaze to Daniel. "If this meets with your approval, Belteshazzar."

Daniel lowered himself to the floor and sat with his legs folded underneath him. His eyes now lower than the king's, he felt much more at ease. He smiled. "I would be honored, my king. But my wisdom is not mine alone. My God has blessed me with three friends who are also among your wise men. Might they be allowed to be of assistance to us as I serve you?"

The king agreed. "Let it be recorded, this day." He turned to a guard who rushed behind the throne and returned with a tablet and charcoal writing stick. "Your friends' names?" the king asked, returning his gaze to Daniel.

Daniel spoke, "Hananiah, Mishael, and Aza . . ." He paused and smiled. "You would know them by their Babylonian names. They are Shadrach, Meshach, and Abednego."

"Let it be recorded, this day," the king repeated, "Shadrach, Meshach, and Abednego are to be in charge of all the affairs of the province of Babylon, while Daniel remains in the court of King Nebuchadnezzar." Then, with a twinkle in his eye, he added, "The eternal head of gold!"

Thought Questions: Chapter 9
1. Why did the king like being compared to a head of gold?
2. Why did the king bow in front of Daniel? How did the people respond?
3. Would you like to be one of Daniel's three friends? Why?

Bible Adventurer Bonus:

You can read this story in Daniel 2.

Chapter 10
Kingdom Stones

King Nebuchadnezzar looked at the captain of his guard, Arioch, and nodded, "Take Belteshazzar to his new rooms."

Arioch raised his eyebrows, as if to say, *Where?* but the king answered before the question was verbalized. "Clear out that group of false prophets from their palace rooms and give the entire area to Belteshazzar and his three associates."

Arioch nodded, placed his huge hand on Daniel's back, and said, "Come with me, sir."

The two men walked to the far end of the room, where they had first entered this morning, and left the king's presence. King Nebuchadnezzar breathed a deep sigh of relief. Then, to no one in particular, he said, "I feel like I could sleep for a week." Then, to his guards, he said, "I am feeling much better now. I'm going to bed. Do not allow anyone to interrupt my sleep!"

The two guards stomped their feet and saluted their king. Nebuchadnezzar slid to the front of his throne, stood, and walked to the doorway he had entered earlier. The two guards followed and stopped at the door, spinning around to guard the entrance.

"Wow!" James said. "Daniel just got himself and his three friends into the most powerful positions in Babylon!"

"Who got him there?" Paul asked, turning to face his brother.

"God did!" Hannah answered before James could.

"That's right," Paul said. "What an amazing God! Daniel said that God gave that dream to the king. Isn't that cool that God can give dreams to people who don't even believe in Him?"

"He loves us all," James said. "Why would He play favorites and only give help to those who know about Him? It's not like Nebuchadnezzar could have known the God of the Hebrews. He was a Babylonian."

"He knows about God now!" Hannah said with a laugh. The three kids had formed a circle as they talked.

Paul pulled out the kingdom scroll card and studied it carefully. His eyebrows furrowed together, and he lifted the card close to his nose. He pushed his glasses closer to his eyes and scrutinized the card. *Hmmph,* he murmured.

"What?" James asked.

"Is there a new line on the card?" Hannah asked.

Paul continued studying the card. "Yes. But there's some weird symbol next to it."

"Show it to us," Hannah said.

Paul turned the kingdom scroll card to face his siblings. "See, it says, 'Kingdom Stones' underneath the first line of 'A Kingdom Dream.'"

Paul held the card steady as his younger siblings studied the new line.

"Oh, I see the symbol," James said excitedly.

Hannah clapped her hands twice. "So do I! It looks like a recycling symbol."

"What do you mean?" Paul asked, looking at the card again.

James and Hannah stood alongside Paul so they could see the card together.

"It looks like a circle to me," James said.

"Not a perfect circle," Paul corrected. "It's oblong—stretched at the ends."

The Kingdom Scroll

"And there's a dot at each end," James said.

"Wait," Hannah said, as she leaned close to examine the circle carefully. "The lines are arrows pointing at the dots. See the little pointy bits at the ends?"

"Oh, yeah!" James said. "The top line points from the first dot to the second. And the bottom line points from the second dot back to the first." Hannah was thinking out loud, "Maybe, it's saying to go from here to there, then come back here."

"Maybe," James agreed.

"That still doesn't tell us what it means," Paul said, scratching his head. "What are we supposed to do?"

"Let's just touch the new line and see what story we go into," James said. "Maybe we will figure the symbol out when we get into the story with the symbol next to it."

"I guess that will work. Let's do it," Paul said, extending his left index finger and reaching toward the card he held in his right hand.

James and Hannah both reached toward the card, their fingers extended toward the "Kingdom Stones" line.

A thought came into Hannah's mind as her finger neared the card. She said, "What if something—" then all three children's fingers touched the card.

Hannah finished her sentence, "weird happens?" The card disappeared. Hannah lifted her eyes from where the card had been to look at Paul. He was gone. Confused, she looked to the left where James had been. He was gone too. She was alone!

She scanned her surroundings and realized the Babylonian palace was also gone. She was still facing a huge marble wall, but she was standing outside.

Suddenly, a male voice cut through the silence. "It's gotta be around here somewhere."

Hannah froze. She didn't recognize the voice.

"It wouldn't be way out here, would it?" another male voice asked.

Kingdom Stones

The voices were not her brothers' voices. They were grown men's voices. But Hannah couldn't see the men.

Next to her, a huge block of marble—the same marble the wall was made of—blocked her view of whom the voices belonged to.

"The quarry master said he sent it to the temple months ago," the first voice said.

Hannah didn't move. She began to shiver, even though she wasn't cold. One repeated thought kept running through her mind, *Where are Paul and James?*

"How could the cornerstone not be in place already?" the second voice asked. They were getting closer. "The quarry master said he sent it the day it was requested."

"Hey," the first voice said, "what about that block?"

"Yeah, it looks about the right size." The two men's voices came closer to Hannah, the marble stone still between them.

The sound of a hand slapping stone filled the air. "This has got to be it!" The two men began walking around the block.

Hannah hadn't moved since her brothers disappeared. The men were coming around the stone. She felt like she should run, but she was so afraid she stayed frozen, like a marble statue.

One of the men came around the corner of the block, not noticing Hannah. He stopped and explored a mark on the side of the stone. "This can't be it," he said.

The other man now came around the corner and joined him. "Why do you say that?"

"This stone has been rejected," he said, pointing at the mark. "The builders put it out here because it didn't fit anywhere inside. And they put a mark on it so they wouldn't make the same mistake again. They probably got tired of it getting in the way. It is huge!"

"Odd," the first man said. "It looks like a perfect match. What were the dimensions again?"

The other man pulled a piece of faded parchment from his satchel

The Kingdom Scroll

and held it against the stone. The two men studied it carefully. Then they measured the stone with their hands, pacing around each side of the massive marble block.

"This is it," the first man said confidently. Then with a laugh, he added, "Can you believe the builders rejected the cornerstone?"

The second man joined in the laughter. "We better go tell the boss."

The two men left together, around the far end of the stone. Their voices faded into the distance. Hannah released a breath of relief. She knew they couldn't see her, but it was scary being alone. The two men and their conversation had distracted her from her loneliness. Now it flooded back like a tidal wave.

Hannah's eyes were fixed on the mark the builders made on the stone to say that they didn't want it. It was a big black X, probably made with a piece of charcoal. Suddenly, the massive marble cornerstone popped like a balloon.

Hannah blinked in amazement and was even more amazed to realize she was no longer looking at the mark, but at the scroll card instead. She could see the line "Kingdom Stones" and the funny symbol.

Hannah raised her eyes from the card and was overjoyed to see Paul and James staring at her.

Thought Questions: Chapter 10
1. Does God tell only His special people about His plans? Why?
2. Why did the builders reject the stone? Was that a good decision? Why?
3. What was the meaning of the symbol on the scroll card?

Bible Adventurer Bonus:

Explore the cornerstone in Psalm 118:22, 23;

Matthew 21:42; and Acts 4:11, 12.

Chapter 11

Five Stones

James's finger was almost touching the line on the scroll card that read "Kingdom Stones" when he heard Hannah say, "What if something—" Then their fingers touched the card.

He looked up at Hannah as she spoke and was amazed to see her disappear right before his eyes. Her voice floated through the empty air even after she was gone. The end of her sentence came through ominously, "weird happens?"

James blinked. The room had changed drastically. The marble walls had turned into tent fabric. The sunlight, which had been pouring in from the overhead windows, now entered the space through an open flap in one tent wall.

"Where are we?" James asked, turning to where Paul had been standing only a moment before.

Nobody answered because nobody was there.

James spun in a circle, exploring the tent. It was empty. "Where are Hannah and Paul?" he asked nobody in particular.

Voices approached from outside the tent. "Come in here, son," a ragged voice said. The flap opened wider, and light filled the tent. James realized he was standing in a corner, behind an equipment rack.

A bearded man, dressed in flowing regal robes, entered the tent and

The Kingdom Scroll

held the flap open for another man. A baby-faced, but very fit, young man walked under the older man's arm and went to the center of the tent.

"You really believe you can defeat the giant?" the older man asked. "Have you had a look at him?"

"I don't need to look at him," the young man said. "I've heard enough. He dares to insult our God. He must die!"

"I agree," the older man said, "but surely a seasoned soldier would be more fitting to face him. I applaud your bravery, but whoever loses this one-on-one battle will lose the battle for their entire kingdom." He folded his muscled arms across his chest.

"My king," the young man said, "while protecting my father's sheep, I have chased down both bears and lions when they stole sheep. When I caught up with the beasts, I hit them with my stick. When they turned on me, I grabbed them by their fur and beat them to death!" The young man made fists and drove them repeatedly into an imaginary beast. "This arrogant Philistine will be like one of those beasts because he insults the Living God."

Clearly impressed, the king said, "Go!" He gestured toward the door and the battlefield beyond. "And, young David, may the Lord be with you."

David turned to walk out of the tent but was stopped by the king. "Wait, you will need armor. I have the best armor in the land!"

The king walked toward where James was standing and stopped at the equipment rack. He lifted a tunic off a peg. "Come, my boy."

David approached the king. He removed his shepherd's cloak and put the tunic over his head. Next, the king picked up a coat of armor, turned, and placed it on David, fixing it in place. It looked heavy—and a bit too big, as the king was quite a bit taller than David. Finally, the king took a huge bronze helmet off the rack and placed it on David's head.

David strapped on his sword and walked in a couple of slow circles.

Five Stones

He squatted and stood, lunged, and tried to draw his sword. The bronze helmet shook from side to side. "It's no good," David said. "I cannot go in these because I am not used to them." David took off each item and returned them to the hands of the king, who placed them back on the rack.

Moments later, David stood wearing his shepherd's cloak and holding his staff in one hand, his sword fixed to his hip. "I will face Goliath as I have faced every other enemy—with the Lord's protection," David said.

The king nodded, "Very well, young warrior. Fight well!"

David walked to the entrance of the tent and headed into the light. The king followed closely behind. James came out from behind the equipment rack. He was so caught up in the story, he had forgotten he was alone. Or, at least, he had put the thought out of his mind.

As they emerged from the tent into the blazing midday sun, David turned toward the hillside where the Israelite army stood and began to run.

James ran after him. He didn't want to miss what would happen next. He already knew the story, but he was excited to see it happen. James ran as fast as he could, trying to catch up with David. No matter how hard he ran, he could only get close enough to see David's back as he wove between soldiers and around fires and weapon racks. "He is fast," James said under his breath as he sprinted after David.

David, with James not far behind, sprinted over the brow of the hill. He picked up more speed as he went downhill. James was amazed. He was always the fastest runner at school, but David was like a cheetah!

David slowed as he neared a small stream. He came to a halt and knelt at the edge of the water. James tucked his head into his chest and sprinted the final leg of the chase. When James got there, David was running his hands over the stones at the edge of the stream. James noticed they were at a bend in the river where the stones had all been pushed into one area.

Slowly, one by one, David chose five stones. He spread the five stones out in his hand and looked at them carefully. He picked up each one in his right hand and weighed it, tossed it in the air, and caught it. Finally, he selected one and put the other four in the leather pouch strapped across his chest.

Untying a knot in another leather cord that ran alongside the pouch, David removed what looked like one long piece of leather string with a pocket in the middle. James realized it was the sling he would use to propel the stone at Goliath.

David stood and looked across the battlefield. James was still standing on the raised bank of the stream and didn't have to wonder what David was looking at. A huge giant stood behind a smaller man who held a massive shield. They were staring at David.

David walked up the other side of the riverbank and leaned against his staff, staring at the giant. James walked across the stream and stood next to him.

The giant, seeing David's staff, shouted, "Am I a dog, that you come at me with sticks? Come here, and I'll give your flesh to the birds and the wild animals!"

David laughed to himself and said under his breath, "He has no idea." Then raising his voice loud enough for both armies to hear, David shouted, "You come against me with sword and spear and javelin, but I come against you in the name of the Lord Almighty, the God of the armies of Israel, whom you have defied. This day the Lord will deliver you into my hands, and I'll strike you down and cut off your head. This very day I will give the carcasses of the Philistine army to the birds and the wild animals, and the whole world will see that there is a God in Israel."

Then David ran—right toward the giant who was now laughing at him.

James shook his head, "God may give him his bravery, but where does he get all his energy?" James took three quick breaths and sprinted toward David and Goliath.

Thought Questions: Chapter 11
1. What story has James gone into? What will happen next?
2. Why did David want to kill Goliath?
3. Why didn't David wear the king's armor? How will David be protected?

Bible Adventurer Bonus:

You can read this story in 1 Samuel 17.

Chapter 12
Two Stone Slabs

Paul held the scroll card in front of him with his right hand. He watched as his left index finger was joined by the fingers of his brother and sister. In just a moment they would be catapulted to a different story in the Bible. He heard Hannah say, "What if something—"

As the three fingers touched the card, a ferociously bright light blazed into existence in front of Paul and cast a hot, white glare into his eyes. As he threw his hands in front of his face, he heard Hannah's voice finish her sentence, "weird happens?"

Paul could feel a dry wind blowing sand against his skin. The wind was coming directly toward him—from where the hot light was. Slowly, he parted his fingers and stared in wonder at a massive wall of fire. The fire was roaring and the wind was like a hurricane, yet the fire stood still, not moved by the wind.

A thunderclap, carried by the wind, burst from the middle of the fire and went through Paul like a wave of dry water. It propelled him backward a few paces. He felt it more than heard it; yet, in some weird way, he understood it. The thunder carried words with it, or in it, or on it, or something.

In the clap of thunder, Paul clearly heard, "I am the Lord your God, who rescued you from the land of Egypt, the place of your slavery. You

Two Stone Slabs

must not have any other god but Me."

How all of that could have been encapsulated in one clap of thunder, which lasted for no more than a second and felt like a kick to the gut, Paul had no idea.

Now that his eyes had fully adjusted, Paul saw a man standing between him and the fire and holding two stone slabs. He looked around to his left and right and behind him and saw a huge gathering of people, all standing in stunned silence, staring at the wall of fire. He couldn't see James or Hannah anywhere.

Suddenly, another clap of thunder whipped from the wall of fire and pulsed through Paul. This one said, "You must not make for yourself any idols. You must not bow down to them or worship them, for I, the Lord your God, am a jealous God."

Again Paul was hurled backward. He slammed into a rock next to the people in the front row of the crowd. From this distance, Paul could see that what had looked like a wall of fire when up close, was actually a pillar of fire reaching from the ground up into stormy black clouds far above their heads. Paul's eyes darted around the crowd, looking for his brother and sister.

Another pulse of word-embedded thunder ripped through Paul and the people standing with him. It said, "You must not misuse the name of the Lord your God."

Paul had been so overwhelmed by the Pillar of fire, the wind, and the ferocious thunderclaps that he hadn't even tried to figure out where he was. Now he didn't need to figure it out. He knew. He was in the Sinai Desert. The man in front of him, with the stone slabs in his hands, was Moses holding the Ten Commandments. The Pillar of fire that was hurling wind and flinging thunder at them was God. And the words carried on the wind and in the thunder from the raging Pillar of fire—from God—were the Ten Commandments.

Another burst of God's law thundered through Paul and the people. God said, "Observe the Sabbath day by keeping it holy." This time Paul felt the clap of thunder, but he wasn't pushed backward. The mass of people absorbed the sound and wind, diminishing its physical force.

A small boy broke through the crowd and stood in front of Paul, crying in fear. A man rushed out of the crowd behind the boy and picked him up. "Here I am, son," the man yelled over the wind. The little boy threw his arms around his father's neck as the next clap of thunder ripped through the people. It said, "Honor your father and mother. Then you will live a long, full life in the land the Lord your God is giving you."

Paul turned to see the man fighting his way back into the crowd, trying to get his son away from the thundering Voice. Suddenly, a sound like firecrackers popping, but with the same intensity of the previous thunder, pulsed from the Pillar of fire. Each pulse had a short demand laced in its thunder.

Clap! "You must not murder."

Bang! "You must not commit adultery."

Thump! "You must not steal."

Thud! "You must not tell lies about other people."

Boom! "You must not wish to take anything that belongs to someone else."

Paul felt like a punching bag that had just taken five of the best hits a prizefighter could unleash. He staggered and fell, then stood back up. Paul scanned the crowd and saw many people had fallen, and others were clinging to and leaning on each other.

Paul waited for another clap of thunder, but none came. *Was that all Ten Commandments?* he wondered. He scanned the crowd again, looking for any sign of Hannah or James. *Where are they?* As his gaze returned to the front, Paul watched in awe as the Pillar of fire backed away from Moses and the people. Standing where the Pillar of fire had been, the tabernacle—God's tent—sat in silent splendor.

After some time, a group of three elderly men emerged from the crowd and walked toward Moses. Paul followed them, wondering what they were going to say. Halfway between the crowd and Moses, Paul

Two Stone Slabs

noticed two footprints, deeply embedded in the desert floor. He stopped to examine them. *Perhaps they were made after a rain, when the ground was muddy,* Paul thought. *But why is there only one set? They don't lead anywhere.*

The group of men was getting ahead of Paul. He ran after them. They reached Moses and gathered around him. Moses greeted them with a smile. He still held the two stone slabs in his hands. The first man stepped forward and said to Moses, "The Lord our God has shown us His glory and greatness, and we have heard His voice from the heart of the fire."

Another man stepped forward and added, "Today we have seen that God can speak to us humans, and yet we live! But now, why should we risk death again? If the Lord our God speaks to us again, we will certainly die and be consumed by this awesome fire."

The third man joined them, stepping forward before he spoke. "Can any living thing hear the voice of the living God from the heart of the fire as we did and yet survive?"

The first man, obviously the leader, finished by saying, "Go yourself and listen to what the Lord our God says. Then come and tell us everything He tells you, and we will listen and obey."

Moses slowly nodded his head. "I will consult with the Lord regarding your request." Moses turned and walked into the tabernacle. The three men exchanged serious glances with each other and stood in silence while awaiting the Lord's answer.

Paul was amazed by their request. *They don't want to hear God's voice anymore?* He wondered what Dad would do if his three kids said to their Mom, "Dad's got a scary voice. Can you please tell him to talk to you and then you tell us what he says? He scares us. But you seem to like talking to him."

Dad would be devastated, Paul thought. *I wonder what answer God will give!*

Thought Questions: Chapter 12

1. What do you think it would be like to hear God speak the Ten Commandments?
2. How many of the Ten Commandments can you remember? List them.
3. How do you think God will respond to the request that He speak to Moses, but not to the people?

Bible Adventurer Bonus:

You can read this story in Deuteronomy 5.

Chapter 13
A Stone's Throw

As David ran, his hand holding the stone found his other hand, which held the two ends of the sling. Quickly, he drew the length of the sling tight in front of him, his eyes fixed on the face of Goliath. He tucked the stone into the pouch and let go. He began swinging the sling in circles as he ran full speed toward the giant.

James sprinted behind David, putting every bit of energy he could muster into keeping up. He saw the sling start to spin. Then he saw David lunge forward; the sling cracked loudly as it whipped toward the giant and launched the stone. David put the full force of his strength and every bit of his momentum into the action. The stone flew like a rocket, directly toward the giant. David took two or three stuttered steps and then stopped, panting heavily as he watched the trajectory of the stone.

James caught up with David and fell to the ground, trying to regain his breath. He had never run that fast in his entire life. From the ground, where he lay on his back, James looked up at David just in time to see him pump his fist in the air and let out a whoop of triumph. James flipped over and jumped to his feet.

The giant was drunkenly staggering backward and forward, to the left and right. His shield bearer had spun around when he heard the wet thud of the stone striking Goliath's skull, and watched in horror as the

The Kingdom Scroll

behemoth of a man stumbled and fell on his face. The shield bearer turned his gaze back to David.

David locked eyes with the shield bearer and reached into his satchel. He shouted menacingly, "I've got a little present for you too!" His hand came out of the satchel holding a stone. He placed the stone in the sling. The huge shield wobbled and then fell to the ground as the man who had been holding it ran for his life.

David put the stone back in his satchel as he walked toward the fallen giant. James walked alongside David. He could feel energy and passion coming from the young shepherd. This moment marked the beginning of a great warrior!

Soon they were standing next to Goliath's massive body. His helmet had come off when he fell to the ground. James could see the hole where the stone had burrowed its way into Goliath's huge skull. David knelt down, placing a hand in front of the giant's nostrils. David said under his breath, "He still lives!"

David reached down and took hold of the hilt of the giant's large sword. He pulled with the full weight of his body, and the sword slid free from its scabbard. David stood and fully withdrew the sword, holding it over his head. With all of his strength, David swung the giant's own sword toward his exposed neck.

Seconds later, David turned toward the armies of Israel and thrust the massive head of Goliath into the air. He shouted, "Victory for the Lord and for Israel!" The two armies, who had all come to the edges of their respective hillsides to watch the duel, moved into action. The Philistine army turned and ran as fast as they could away from the Israelites. The Israelite army took up the chase.

David and James stood and watched as the army of Israel rushed toward them. Hundreds of armored soldiers ran past, many of them shouting words of congratulations to their new hero. David took the head and sword of Goliath and began walking back to the camp of the Israelite army. His job for the day was finished.

A Stone's Throw

James walked next to David. *I wish I could talk to him,* James thought as he studied David's face. *It would be so awesome to ask him, "Were you afraid, even a little bit? Did you consider what would happen if the stone missed? Why did you take five stones?"* As James considered the many questions he would like to ask, he again realized that he was alone.

What happened to Paul and Hannah? James wondered. *Where are they? Did they stay in Babylon and only I came to the battlefield?* Question after question paraded through James's mind. And the most frightening question of all was, *How do I get back to them without the scroll card?*

David and James went over the top of the hill and into the Israelite camp. The king was standing in the center of the camp. When he saw David, he saluted him. "Well done, great warrior!"

"Thank you, my king," David said, bowing to one knee. He offered Goliath's head and sword to the king. "These are for you, my king."

"You keep them," the king answered. "You've earned them! You've also earned the right to call me by name."

"Thank you, my king," David answered. "I mean, King Saul."

The king laughed. "You're a good kid, David. I'm sure God has great plans for you!" King Saul gestured at Goliath's head and sword, "Go put those in your tent and then come find me in my tent. Tonight, we celebrate!"

"Um, s-sir," David stuttered. "I am not a soldier. I don't have a tent."

"Your father has many sons in this army," King Saul replied. "Their tent is your tent! You may have started the day as a shepherd, but you've finished it as a soldier."

David nodded and ducked into one of the nearby tents. King Saul wandered to the far end of the camp and entered a large tent with flags in front of it.

James stood watching as the two men left him. Again, he realized, *I am alone.* A shiver of fear ran up his spine.

David came back out of the tent, muttering under his breath, "I'm glad my brothers have a tent, or I'd have to carry that disgusting head around with me all night!" He jogged toward King Saul's tent.

James watched him go. He could follow him, but he had lost interest in what David was doing. The more he tried not to think about being alone and stuck in ancient Israel, the more he could think of nothing else. *How am I going to get out of here?*

He turned in a slow circle, looking for something—anything. *Perhaps Paul and Hannah are somewhere nearby. Maybe they are in one of the tents. What if they had run with the soldiers, chasing the Philistines? Perhaps they are still in Babylon. If that's the case,* James thought, *I'm stuck. No scroll card. No hints. No help.*

James began wandering randomly through the tents. Even though he knew where he was, he felt lost—lost and alone.

Thought Questions: Chapter 13
1. Was Goliath scared at all? Was this wise? Why?
2. How do you think David felt after killing the giant?
3. How will James get back to Paul and Hannah?

Bible Adventurer Bonus:
You can read this story in 1 Samuel 17.

Chapter 14
Kingdom Builders

Moses emerged from the tabernacle just a few minutes after he had entered.

That must have been an easy question for God to answer, Paul thought. *I'm sure He wants everyone, not just Moses, to hear His voice.*

Moses approached the three elders and spoke, "The Lord heard your request and He said, 'I have heard what the people said to you, and they are right.'"

An audible sigh of relief came from the three elders.

Paul was amazed. *Right! Right?* he wondered. *How could God think it was a good idea for people to not hear His voice?* Paul wished James and Hannah were here to talk to. *Where are they, anyway?* he wondered, beginning to get worried.

"God was impressed by your request," Moses continued. "Fear of the Lord is the beginning of wisdom."

The three men nodded.

Moses said, "God has asked me to send you back to your tents while I return to His presence, and He will explain His law and all He wishes for us to become."

One of the elders said, "We will lead the people back to their tents. Call for us when you are ready to tell us what the Lord commands. We will obey!" The other two men nodded in agreement.

Moses smiled. "That is all God asks."

The three men walked toward the crowd. Moses watched for a moment and then turned and went back into God's tent. In a moment of bravery, Paul decided to follow Moses. He walked to the tent flap and slipped inside the tabernacle.

A bright light filled the room. There was a curtain between this room, called the Holy Place, and the next room, called the Most Holy Place. Paul knew there was only one day a year when God's leader could enter the Most Holy Place. That room was filled with the presence of God, and the ark of the covenant was kept there.

Moses stood in the middle of the Holy Place, facing the light that seemed to emanate from the curtain. Clearly, the presence of God was on the other side of the curtain!

Moses said, "I have returned to hear Your commands, decrees, and regulations."

A Voice said, "You must tell them to carefully obey all the commands of the Lord their God." The Voice seemed to come from the center of the curtain, but it also seemed to be all around them.

Paul recognized the Voice. It was the same Voice that had spoken in the thunder, or on the wind, or however it worked—the Voice that had declared the Ten Commandments. But this time it was a gentle, embracing, and compelling voice. Paul now understood why Moses enjoyed talking to God. *And, perhaps, this is why God prefers to talk to one person*, Paul thought. *He can use His indoor voice!*

"Tell them," God continued, "they must obey these laws both now and in the land I have promised them. Their children and grandchildren must respect Me and obey My laws. If they do, they will enjoy a long life!"

Paul wondered if that was a threat or a promise. *Probably a promise*, he decided. *God's laws make us healthy and happy. So, if we follow them, we live longer, happier lives.*

"Tell them," the Voice said, "there is only one God. They must love

Me and Me alone. They must love Me with all of their hearts, all of their souls, and all of their strength. And they must give My commands their full attention, every day."

Moses was listening carefully, nodding his head after every proclamation. Somehow, it had escaped Paul's notice until now that Moses was no longer holding the two stone slabs. Paul looked around the room and could not see them anywhere. *They must be in the ark already,* Paul thought. *God must have taken them when Moses entered the tent to ask the elders' question.*

Moses lowered his head and spoke, "May I ask a question, my Lord and King?"

"Yes," came the resonant reply.

"How should Your people," Moses chose his words carefully, "spend their days? You have said You wish for them to give their full attention to Your commands with all their hearts and souls and strength. What is the best way they can do this every day, all day long?"

"They must teach My ways to their children," God answered. "They must repeat My laws again and again to the young. A love that is full strength in adulthood is formed in childhood. Tell the parents to talk about Me and My ways when they are at home and when they are on the road, when they are going to bed and when they are getting up. Tell them to use questions and stories to connect My laws to everything they do with their hands, everything they say with their mouths, and everything they think about. Tell them to write My laws on the doorposts of their houses and on their gates."

Moses listened carefully and then responded, "I will tell them. Parents seem to be very important to You!"

"Parents are My kingdom builders!" the Voice said. "In the future, every generation of children will ask, 'What is the meaning of these laws, decrees, and regulations that the Lord our God has commanded us to obey?' If the parents and grandparents have told My story well and lived My law joyfully, their children will know what to say to the next generation. Tell them, Moses!"

The Kingdom Scroll

"I will, my Lord," Moses said. "I will." The light coming through the curtain faded to a dim glow. As Moses turned, Paul noticed his face was glowing. Standing in the presence of God's glory had caused Moses to radiate like the moon that reflects the light of the sun. Moses made his way out of the tabernacle to speak to the people of Israel.

Paul stood alone. Now that the blazing light had subsided, Paul recognized the Holy Place furniture from his first journey into the Bible with the serpent scroll. The seven-branched lampstand was on one wall. The table of shewbread was on the other. And near the curtain separating the Holy Place from the Most Holy Place, some incense sent smoke heavenward, like the prayers of the people.

Paul wished Hannah and James were here to talk to. He had so many questions. So many ideas. *Where are they? What has happened? How did we become separated? How will we get back together?*

Paul took the kingdom scroll card out of his pocket and examined it. There was nothing new. The final line still read "Kingdom Stones," and that weird little symbol was still there. Paul pointed his finger and touched the card. Nothing happened. He touched the words *Kingdom Stones*. Nothing happened. He touched the little symbol. Again, nothing happened.

He was stuck. And he was alone. What scared Paul even more than being stuck alone in the desert was the realization that James and Hannah were probably stuck alone too. *What will they do? Will they be all right?*

Kingdom Builders

Thought Questions: Chapter 14

1. Why was God willing to talk to the people through Moses?
2. Who are God's kingdom builders? How do parents build God's kingdom?
3. Why does God want us to tell His story? What impact will it have on our friends and family?

Bible Adventurer Bonus:

You can read this story in Deuteronomy 6.

Chapter 15
Retracing Steps

James stuck his head in yet another tent and looked around. No Paul. No Hannah.

"Obviously, they aren't here," James muttered to himself. "There must be some way to get back."

He decided to replay the story, looking for clues. "*Hmmm,*" James said out loud as he scanned the rows of tents, "Which tent is the one with Saul's armor in it?" His eyes focused on a normal army tent next to King Saul's special tent with the flags out front. The little rough-looking tent would be the perfect place for the king's armor. James ran toward the tent.

He stuck his head through the tent flap but couldn't tell what was inside. He entered the tent and, once his eyes had adjusted to the darkness, began to recognize things. He had found the right tent! Carefully, James explored the room. He walked from object to object. There was the king's armor, hanging from pegs. The sword and shield leaned against the equipment rack James had been standing behind when he had first arrived.

It looked exactly the same as it had before. There was nothing new. No way to get back to Paul and Hannah. James had been hoping he would see something obvious, such as a shining blue portal or a black hole on the ground he could jump through like in a computer game.

Retracing Steps

James scratched his head in consternation.

* * * * *

More than anything else, Paul wanted to get to Hannah and James. The thought of them being trapped and alone made him very distressed. *How can I get out of here?*

The kingdom scroll card hadn't helped. Maybe there was some clue around the tabernacle. Paul carefully looked around the Holy Place one last time before leaving through the tent flap. He began walking toward the tabernacle courtyard. A few paces outside the tabernacle he spun in a full circle, looking for a clue as to what he should do next.

Behind God's tent, Paul saw the Pillar of fire raging. The impressive heat and light coming from the Pillar gave the entire tabernacle a kind of wavering effect—like heat waves rising off the road on a hot summer day.

Next to the tent was a mountain. It wasn't a huge mountain, but it did stand out due to the flatness of everything else in the desert. A trail of dusty footprints led to a path heading up the side of the mountain. *That must be Mount Sinai,* Paul thought, *where God gave the Ten Commandments to Moses.*

The entrance to the tabernacle met up with the trailhead that went up the mountain. Around the base of the mountain was a large buffer space; at some distance away, the tents of the Israelites stretched as far as the eye could see in every direction.

Paul was baffled and confused. "What's going on?" he said. "I've tried everything."

* * * * *

James decided to go for a run. Sometimes running helped to clear his mind. He decided to run to all of the places he and David had been. He ran out of the king's armor tent and toward the battlefield.

Coming over the crest of a hill, he sprinted down to the stream where David had picked up five smooth stones. He stopped and explored the area. There was nothing obvious to tell him how to get back to Paul and Hannah.

He ran to the body of Goliath. Again, there was nothing of any help.

James threw his arms open wide and yelled to the sky, "What am I supposed to do?"

No answer came. So, he ran back to the Israelite camp, trying to take the same path David had taken while carrying the head and sword of Goliath.

He stopped where David and King Saul had talked to each other. Nothing.

Soon he was back at King Saul's armor tent. The run had made James tired but had not given him new ideas on how to get out of this place. Breathing hard from the run, he leaned over and put his hands on his knees. "This is crazy!" he muttered in frustration.

* * * * *

Paul walked toward the place where he and the people had heard God's thunder proclaim the Ten Commandments. Perhaps some hint would jump out at him if he replayed the Ten Commandments in his head.

As he walked, he noticed the two footprints again. He stopped to examine them. Embedded in the desert floor, one set of footprints stood alone, directly next to each other, as if the person had been standing still. *Where are the other prints from this person?* Paul wondered. *He or she must have walked somewhere. Or the person would still be standing here.*

Then something extremely obvious leaped out at Paul. How had he missed it? Inside each footprint was a pattern—wavy lines with a logo—made by the sole of a shoe. *Were the sandals worn by the Israelites made with patterned soles like modern shoes?* Paul wondered. *Surely not!*

Retracing Steps

Paul lifted one of his feet and looked at the bottom of his shoe. There, staring back at him, were wavy lines with a logo in the middle.

"They are my footprints?" Paul asked in amazement. He carefully placed his right foot in the right footprint. It fit like a glove—or a shoe, to be more precise. He lifted his left foot and snapped it into the left print.

* * * * *

James walked back into the king's armory, this time determined to find something.

He lifted each piece of the king's armor and examined it. He looked inside the helmet. He tried on the body armor. He lifted the sword and swung it a couple of times. It was heavy! He examined the king's shield, letting his fingers follow the patterns on both of its sides. Each thing found unhelpful went back into its place.

After exploring all of the obvious stuff, James saw an unlit torch on the far tent wall. He went over to it and noticed a piece of flint dangling on a string from the handle. He took the torch down and struck the flint against the metal cap at the top of the torch. Strips of rag, wrapped just below and hung over the top, burst into a gentle flame.

The transformation in the room was amazing. James could see little tools hanging from the side walls, jugs lining the bottom of the walls, and the sword and shield glinted and gleamed in the torchlight. James walked over to the equipment rack. He studied the inscription on the sword's hilt. As he leaned in toward the sword, he noticed something on the ground on the other side of the rack. He walked around the equipment rack and knelt down in the corner of the tent to examine two footprints embedded in the soil.

"They look too small to be a soldier's footprints," James muttered to himself. "Why are they so deep in the ground?" He ran his finger around the edge of one of the footprints. Laying the torch down next to the footprints, he sat cross-legged and removed one of his shoes. He gently placed the shoe on the matching footprint and was amazed to see it fit perfectly.

James put his shoe back on excitedly. He rolled the torch around on the ground and put it out. Then, standing up, he carefully stepped into one footprint and then the other. His feet clicked into place.

The ground changed colors from dirt brown to marble white. James realized he was looking at the kingdom scroll card. He looked up and was overjoyed to see Hannah and Paul, who were looking overjoyed right back at him.

Thought Questions: Chapter 15

1. Have you ever looked at your own footprint? What is special about it?
2. Have you ever been stuck in your thinking? What steps can you take to get free?
3. Do you think the kids were excited to see each other again? Why?

Chapter 16

Together Again

Hannah spoke first, "Hey guys! That was cool, wasn't it?"

Paul and James stared at her, both trying to decide if they should be honest or pretend to be as relaxed as Hannah.

James answered, "Uh, at first, yeah. But then it was really scary. I thought I was never going to get back."

Paul said, "Me too. I was so afraid I would never find you guys again."

Hannah looked from one brother to the other. "What do you mean? We were gone for only a couple of minutes."

"A couple of minutes!" James nearly shouted. "I was there for hours."

"Yeah," Paul added, "I thought I was going to wander with Moses in the desert for forty years!"

"Moses?" both Hannah and James said together.

"Don't you mean David?" James asked.

"David?" Hannah said. "There was just a big rock and a couple of workmen."

The reality of what had happened hit all three of them at the same time.

"We went to different places!" they said together.

"Where did you go?" Hannah asked, looking at James. "What was King David doing?"

The Kingdom Scroll

"He wasn't a king yet," James said. "It was when he killed Goliath. I watched it all happen!"

"Wow!" Hannah laughed. "What about you, Paul? What story did you see?"

"It was the story of the Ten Commandments being given," Paul said. "But it was very different from what I remember studying."

"What do you mean?" James said. "Didn't Moses come down the mountain holding the tablets and see the people dancing around the golden calf and get so angry that he chucked the tablets on the ground?"

"Nope," Paul answered. "God spoke each commandment in thunder."

"That's not in the Bible," Hannah said confidently.

"It was weird," Paul said. "The people asked God not to talk to them anymore. And God said OK, and then He said parents need to tell their children about Him and His law."

James raised his hand and started talking at the same time, "I know that story!" The other two looked at him with interest. "At church a few weeks ago, the pastor told that story. It's in Deuteronomy, I think."

"But, I thought," Paul said, "the Ten Commandments are in Exodus chapter twenty. That's what we learned when we memorized them at church."

"Maybe the story is told twice," Hannah said, "in different books of the Bible."

"Maybe," Paul said. "Weird." Paul looked at Hannah and realized she hadn't said where she went. "Hey, Hannah, what Bible story did you go into?"

"I don't know," Hannah said.

"How can you not know?" James argued. "You were there!"

"I've never heard the story," Hannah said. "And it went by pretty quick. I was standing by a big piece of marble." She pointed to the marble walls around them. "Just like this kind of marble. There was nothing else that I could see. Then two workmen came to the block, talking about it. They were looking for something called the 'cornerstone,' and after looking at my block for a while, they realized it was the one they wanted. They thought it was funny because this stone had been rejected by the builders and the cornerstone is the most important stone in a building."

"That is ironic," James said.

"Jesus talked about that stone," Paul said.

"He did?" Hannah asked.

"Yeah, He said the stone rejected by the builders had become the cornerstone. I think He was talking about Himself."

"Cool," James said.

"People did reject Jesus," Hannah said. "So that makes sense. Everything we believe is built on Him!"

"True," Paul said. "So, how did you get back here, Hannah?"

Hannah looked confused. "I didn't. When the two workmen walked away, I just appeared back here, looking at you two."

"Whoa!" James said, "You had it easy, baby!"

"She sure did," Paul said. "I wonder why? I had to find my footprints—I didn't know they were special until I stepped in them—but I had to find them in the desert!"

"Me too!" James agreed. "Mine were in the corner of King Saul's armor tent. Once I found them, I guessed what they were for and stepped in them."

"I never moved," Hannah said. "I just zipped in and out."

James said, "You never moved!"

"Your feet were still in your footprints," Paul explained. "That makes perfect sense, now."

"Hey," Hannah said, "that symbol on the scroll card is what did this. We each went to a different story and then came back to the same place. Now we know what the symbol means. Next time we will know what's about to happen!"

"I'll take a careful look at my footprints before I go running off," James said. "So I remember where to come back to!"

The Kingdom Scroll

Paul was lost in his thoughts while the other two talked. When they saw the look in his eyes, the other two grew quiet.

"What is it?" Hannah asked.

"I'm just wondering what these three stories have to do with God's kingdom?" Paul said.

"The title for that section was 'Kingdom Stones,'" James said. "So maybe it was more about stones than the kingdom."

"I saw a stone," Hannah said. "And Paul saw stones. But you didn't." She was looking at James.

"Yes, I did. I saw five of them!"

"Oh, yeah," Hannah laughed. "So we all saw different kinds of stones."

"And each kind of stone probably teaches us something about God's kingdom," Paul said. "Mine is obvious. God's law is very important to living in God's kingdom. But what about the stones in your stories?"

Hannah said, "Well, like you said, Jesus was rejected just like the cornerstone in my story. So I guess, the lesson would be that we should not reject Jesus when we see Him. He should be the Cornerstone of our lives. Everything should be built on Him."

"Sounds good!" Paul said. "What about you, James? What does the stone in your story teach us about God's kingdom?"

James scratched his head for a minute, "I dunno. We can throw rocks at mean people?"

Hannah laughed.

"I don't think so," Paul said.

"Well," James said, "David was angry at Goliath because he made fun of God. And David used the skills he had to stop the giant from insulting God. I guess we can do the same thing: stop people from mocking God."

"Good one," Paul said.

"That reminds me of a Bible verse we learned at church last week," Hannah said. "'God cannot be mocked. A man reaps what he sows.'

Together Again

Galatians chapter six, verse seven."

James laughed. "Goliath certainly reaped what he sowed!"

"Sure did!" Paul said.

"I think the card wanted us to learn a little extra on a side theme," Hannah said. "So we took steps sideways."

"In a paper for school," Paul said, "it's the kind of thing you'd put in a footnote."

"That explains the footprints!" James said, rubbing his hands together. "We jumped to a footnote and used the footprints to get back to the main study."

"Cool," Hannah said.

"Very cool," the boys said together.

Thought Questions: Chapter 16

1. Why wasn't Hannah scared like the boys?
2. Which of the three stories the kids explored was your favorite? Why?
3. Retell the point the kids learned from each story: the Cornerstone, David and Goliath, and the Ten Commandments.

Chapter 17

Bow or Burn

"Well, we're back in Nebuchadnezzar's palace," James said. "What are we going to do next?"

Paul reached into his pocket to retrieve the kingdom scroll card. But before he could pull out the card, three excited voices filled the throne room.

"We've got to hurry if we want to make it on time," one voice said.

"You're right," another man said. "Mishael always takes so long grooming himself! We are going to miss the chariot, and it's too far to walk!"

"Oh, get over it!" the third man said, obviously Mishael. "I was getting some parchment."

"Parchment?" the other two men said together, as they walked past the children and toward the main entrance to the throne room. Paul, Hannah, and James fell into step behind Daniel's three friends.

"What do you need parchment for? We're going to the Dura Plain; it's the middle of a desert!"

"Hananiah, you know we should always be prepared!" Mishael said, "What if the king asks us to record an edict or some such thing. We need parchment!"

"True enough," Hananiah responded.

Azariah interrupted, "I can't believe we are really going to see a ninety-foot tall statue of gold! Is there really that much gold in the world? I can't wait to see it!"

"It is going to be amazing," Mishael said.

"Too bad Daniel's not here," Hananiah said. "He would love to see the statue."

"He always gets to travel," Mishael replied. "I wish I had half his luck!"

"It's not luck," Azariah interjected. "Daniel is worth his weight in gold. He never makes mistakes, and yet he always puts God first."

"True," the other men said together.

They continued walking and talking until they came to a busy city street. People were streaming out of the city. The three men walked to a chariot waiting by a high wall and climbed in. Hannah, James, and Paul sat on the floor at the men's feet.

A while later, the chariot came to a stop, and the three men stepped on to the sand. The children followed them into a huge crowd. They wove through hundreds of people until the three men found a position they liked. They stopped walking and turned to face the same direction everyone else was facing.

Although it was far away and a sea of people stood in front of them, it was easy to see the massive gold statue and the huge platform it was built on.

"It looks just like the statue in the king's dream," Hannah said.

"Yeah," James agreed. "Its arms are folded across its chest."

"It looks like King Nebuchadnezzar," Paul said, pointing at the king standing center stage, not far from the statue. "There is one major difference between that statue and the one in the dream."

"What?" James blurted.

"It's gold from head to foot!" Paul said.

"Hey," James said, "you're right! Why would he do that?"

"Maybe it was too hard to build it out of lots of different metals," Hannah said.

"No," Paul said. "I don't think Nebuchadnezzar liked the idea of his kingdom coming to an end, so he is trying to rewrite the prophecy by making an all-gold statue!"

"As if that's gonna work!" James laughed. "God is not going to change His plans because a selfish king wants to live forever."

Just then a chorus of horns blasted three short pulses. The crowd became quiet. A herald stepped toward a massive conelike megaphone and shouted, "People of all races and nations and languages, listen to the king's command! When you hear the sound of the musical instruments, bow to the ground to worship King Nebuchadnezzar's gold statue. Anyone who refuses to obey will immediately be thrown into a blazing furnace."

"Oh, I know this story," James said, almost to himself.

"The fiery furnace," Hannah responded.

"Yup," the boys said together. On the left side of the stage, the huge metal smelting furnace, used to make the statue, burned its warning to the people: bow or burn.

Suddenly, a blare of sound came from various instruments on the stage. Thousands of people bowed to the great statue. All bowed except Daniel's three friends.

"Hey, look at those guys over there," James said, pointing at a cluster of men who were on their knees but were looking at Daniel's friends rather than at the statue. They were gesturing and pointing at Hananiah, Mishael, and Azariah. Two of the three men stood and walked to the edge of the crowd and then ran to the stage. They talked to the king for a few moments, pointed into the crowd—directly at the three standing men.

King Nebuchadnezzar stood from his throne and peered into the crowd. It was impossible to hear what he said next, but his body language was clear. His arms flailed up, down, left, and right and then a menacing finger pointed at the three standing men; and Nebuchadnezzar's eyes bore into them. Two soldiers rushed from the stage and into the crowd. They covered the distance quickly and soon stood before Daniel's friends.

"Come with us!" one of the soldiers shouted, "The king wants to talk to you, right now!" The two soldiers led the three men through the crowd, and the three children followed closely behind.

When they finally climbed the stairs and walked on to the stage, Nebuchadnezzar stormed toward them, his face as red as a tomato. He began shouting while he was still walking toward them, "Is it true, Shadrach, Meshach, and Abednego, that you refuse to serve my gods or worship the gold statue I have set up?"

The king didn't wait for an answer to his question, but stormed on with his next statement, "I will give you one more chance to bow down and worship the statue I have made. But if you refuse, you will be thrown immediately into the blazing furnace. And then what god will be able to rescue you from my power?"

The three men looked at each other. It was as if they were having a conversation with their eyes. Finally, Azariah said, "O Nebuchadnezzar, we do not need to defend ourselves before you. If we are thrown into the blazing furnace, the God whom we serve is able to save us."

The king's eyebrows shot up higher than seemed possible. His disbelief was clear and his anger was mounting.

Mishael said, "He will rescue us from your power, Your Majesty."

An evil sneer crossed the king's face. "We'll see about that!"

Then Hananiah said, "But even if our God doesn't rescue us, we want to make it clear to you, Your Majesty, that we will never serve your gods or worship the gold statue you have set up."

That did it. Nebuchadnezzar's rage shot through the roof. Every vein in his neck and head could be seen pulsing with every beat of his enraged heart. He turned to a soldier and said through gritted teeth, "Make the fire seven times hotter!" The soldier quickly ordered servants to throw more fuel into the furnace.

To another group of soldiers, he said, "Tie these traitors with ropes.

And tie them as tight as you can!" When their hands and feet were tied together, the king said, "Now pick them up and throw them in the fire!"

Three massively muscled soldiers lifted Hananiah, Mishael, and Azariah off the ground. They held them sideways, like long planks of wood, and ran toward the fire. With every bit of strength they could muster, the soldiers threw the three men into the flames. Then, because of the severe heat, the soldiers fell to their knees before they could get away from the fire.

"It's so hot," James said, "they can't even move!"

"They are dead," Paul said. "The heat from the fire killed them."

"But what about Daniel's friends?" Hannah asked. "Are they dead too?"

Thought Questions: Chapter 17

1. Why did the king make the statue completely gold? To whom was he being disrespectful by doing this?
2. Would you be able to be as brave as Hananiah, Mishael, and Azariah? Why?
3. Will God rescue them? How?

Bible Adventurer Bonus:

You can read this story in Daniel 3.

Chapter 18
Frozen Worship

Daniel's three friends disappeared into the raging inferno as the soldiers slumped to the ground.

Nebuchadnezzar laughed and turned to the crowd, spitting out the challenge, "Anyone else want to disobey me?"

The people in the first few rows shrunk back in fear. Nebuchadnezzar returned his gaze to the furnace.

From where they stood next to the king, the three children stared into the flames.

"I thought they were supposed to survive," James said. "Doesn't the Bible say they came out of the fire unhurt?"

"Yes," Paul said. "Can't you see it?"

"See what?" Hannah and James said together.

"Keep your eyes on the flames," Paul said. "Let your eyes adjust. Look through the fire."

The three children stared into the fire, as did King Nebuchadnezzar. The flames danced, mesmerizing the children with their power and ferocity.

Suddenly, Nebuchadnezzar turned to his advisers, "Didn't we tie up three men and throw them into the furnace?"

"Yes, Your Majesty, we certainly did," they replied.

"Look!" Nebuchadnezzar shouted. "I see four men, unbound, walking around in the fire unharmed! And the fourth looks like a god!"

"I see it too," Hannah said, clapping her hands in amazement.

"Yeah," James said. Pumping his fist in the air, he yelled, "*Woo-hoo! We won't bow, and we won't burn!*"

"Who is the fourth one?" Hannah asked.

"Look carefully," Paul answered. "I think you'll recognize Him."

Hannah clapped her hands again. "It's Jesus! Jesus is in the fire with them!"

Then Nebuchadnezzar came as close as he could to the entrance of the flaming furnace and shouted, "Shadrach, Meshach, and Abednego, servants of the Most High God, come out! Come here!"

Hananiah, Mishael, and Azariah stepped out of the fire and walked to the king. Everyone on the stage crowded around them and saw that the fire had not touched them.

Hannah, Paul, and James got as close as they could and examined Daniel's three friends. Not a hair on their heads was singed, and their clothing was not scorched. They didn't even smell of smoke!

King Nebuchadnezzar led the three men to the center of the stage, in view of all the people assembled to worship the statue. He stood in front of the massive megaphone and shouted, "Praise to the God of Shadrach, Meshach, and Abednego! He sent His angel to rescue His servants who trusted in Him. They defied my command and were willing to die rather than serve or worship any god except their own God. Therefore, I make this decree: if anyone speaks a word against the God of Shadrach, Meshach, and Abednego, they will be torn limb from limb, and their houses will be turned into heaps of rubble. There is no other god who can rescue like this!"

"As if God needs his help," James said with a laugh.

"What do you mean?" Hannah asked.

"He just said he would tear people to pieces for not worshiping God," James explained. "Even though God is obviously more powerful than he is."

Frozen Worship

"He still wants to be in charge," Paul said. "He's trying to regain his authority by making threats."

"If you can't beat 'em, join 'em!" James said with a laugh.

King Nebuchadnezzar raised his hands to silence every voice. He waited until he had the undivided attention of the entire assembly. He gestured toward the three men standing next to him. "These three men," he shouted, "are already on my advisory council and have authority over all of Babylon. I now decree that they are rulers in this land. Because they have remained true to their God through a test of fire, they are worthy of leadership in Babylon, the greatest nation on earth!"

The people cheered as King Nebuchadnezzar stepped between Azariah and Mishael and wrapped his arms around them. He had turned a negative into a positive. Clearly, he needed this God on his side.

"He sure saved face," James said. "That could have been a real problem if he had not handled it so well."

"I think he was genuinely impressed," Paul said. "I think King Nebuchadnezzar believes their God is truly a powerful God."

"And all because Hananiah, Mishael, and Azariah wouldn't bow to that gold statue," Hannah said, pointing up at the massive statue towering far above them.

James crossed his arms across his chest. "I think Daniel's friends were a bit crazy. They could have died!"

"They were willing to die," Paul said, staring at his brother.

James frowned as Paul spoke. "What's so bad about a big gold statue? I'm sure all the people knew it wasn't really a god. They bowed to it only because they had to."

Paul was amazed that his brother didn't understand. "Nebuchadnezzar was trying to say that all the other nations from his dream were never going to happen. His kingdom was going to last forever. And he was wrong."

James uncrossed his arms and put his hands on his hips. "Yeah, I know. So Nebby was a loony. We know that! But why would it have been so bad for Hananiah, Mishael, and Azariah to bow down? They wouldn't have been really worshiping the statue or the king. They knew neither was a real God."

Paul spread his arms wide as he explained, "Nebuchadnezzar wanted to see everyone bow to his eternal kingdom. He was trying to change the future. God's people could not go along with that. God's law is very clear—His people are never to bow to anything other than Him."

Hannah had been scanning the crowd, the stage, the statue, and the furnace as she listened. Finally, her gaze rested on the king, who was now talking to the three men as if they were long-lost friends. She said, "So, Nebuchadnezzar was stuck in his thinking. He didn't want to admit that God was really the King of everything on earth—including the future."

James lifted one finger high in the air like he was making a point. "That makes sense!" he said excitedly. "The all-gold statue was like frozen thinking. Nebby was stuck—on himself!"

Paul smiled at James's quirky action. "That's why it's wrong to worship any idol, of any type."

Hannah said, "Because they are stuck on themselves?"

Paul pursed his lips in thought. "Well, kind of," he said. "Idols make us stop looking for God. Once you find your god frozen in stone, you stop searching."

"Or frozen in gold!" James said, turning to point at the statue. "That's why God said not even to make statues of Him. He doesn't want us getting stuck—frozen on one view of Him."

Hannah nodded. "Yeah," she said, "He wants us to keep looking for new ways of knowing Him all the time."

"I guess," James said, scratching his head, "living in God's kingdom is not so much about saying, 'Here I stand,' as it is about saying, 'Here we go!'"

"That's cool," Paul said. "Good thought. God wants us to keep following Him, wherever He leads."

Hannah turned toward Paul and stepped closer, "Paul, can you check the scroll card? I wonder if there's somewhere new to go."

"Good idea," Paul said. "I'm ready to get out of here too."

James turned to the crowd and clapped his hands three times, as if he were trying to get their attention. Of course, they couldn't hear him. "My people," James shouted, as if he were making a proclamation, "let us remove ourselves from Babylon!" He turned back to his brother and sister and rubbed his hands together, a cheeky grin on his face.

Paul smiled at his brother. "You're funny, James." Paul pulled the kingdom scroll card from his pocket and held it in front of himself so the other two could see it clearly.

The bottom line of text was new. Paul read it out loud, "Kingdom Children."

"Yes!" James said, "Let's go!"

"I hope we get to see Jesus!" Hannah added.

They each pointed their finger and reached toward the scroll card. Then they touched it.

The world around them blinked off and on rapidly; and then, in a flash of white light, they were on a blank page—nothing but white as far as the eye could see.

Thought Questions: Chapter 18
1. Why did the king demand that everyone worship the God of Hananiah, Mishael, and Azariah?
2. We have a God who is willing to walk in the fire with us. What does this mean to you?
3. How do people today sometimes "freeze" their view of God? How is this like idol worship?

Bible Adventurer Bonus:

You can read this story in Daniel 3.

Chapter 19

Kingdom Children

"Well, everything is white," James said. "Where are we?"

"Do you think Jesus will be in this story?" Hannah asked.

At the sound of His name, Jesus spoke from behind the kids, just a short distance away. "Hey, kids!"

They spun around and saw Jesus sitting on a stump, surrounded by whiteness.

"Jesus?" Hannah said, all smiles. He smiled back and gestured for the kids to approach. Hannah ran toward Jesus. Her brothers were close behind.

"Wow," James shouted, as they ran, "a private visit with Jesus!"

Hannah reached Jesus and climbed up in His lap. "It's so cool that You can see us," she said. "Nobody else in the Bible can."

"True," Jesus said. The boys were now sitting at His feet. "I am always with you. The other people in the Bible stories lived a very long time ago! You can explore their stories, but you can't talk to them. Well, not until you get to heaven."

"That will be so much fun," James said. "I can't wait."

"Soon, My little friend," Jesus said, as He ruffled James's already messy hair.

"Why is everything else still white?" Paul asked.

Kingdom Children

"Good question," James said. "Hannah said Jesus' name, and now He is visible."

"What does the card say again?" Hannah asked.

"Kingdom Children," Paul said. And as he said it, a crowd of children popped into view. They were everywhere. The ground was covered in kids, all pushing to get closer to Jesus. There was a little boy, younger than Hannah, sitting on Jesus' other knee.

Beyond the crowd of children, the world was still white. Just then, a voice called from the whiteness, "Get those kids away from Jesus! He's a busy man!"

"Oh! Oh!" James was jumping on the spot, raising his hand like he was in class. "I know where we are! The disciples are trying to stop children from touching Jesus, even though Jesus wants to see the kids!" He spun to face Jesus, "Right?"

Jesus' eyebrows went up, and He pointed into the distance. Like sand being covered as a wave rolls up on a beach, the whiteness was overwhelmed by a living sea of humanity. There were people everywhere.

A disciple, fighting his way through the crowd, shouted, "Get away! Come on, you useless lot! Jesus has better things to do than cuddle babies!"

A few mothers, lifting their babies toward Jesus over others in the crowd, heard the rebuke and sadly pulled their little ones back to themselves.

Jesus grabbed the disciple who had just fought his way through the crowd and, under His breath, said very sternly, "Let the children come to Me. Don't stop them! For the kingdom of God belongs to those who are like these children."

Jesus wrapped His arms around Hannah and the boy on His other knee. In a big voice, He said loudly, "I tell you the truth, anyone who doesn't receive the kingdom of God like a child will never enter it."

As if to make His point, Jesus kissed Hannah on the top of her head and then did the same to the little boy. Then He set them back on the ground and took another child into His arms to bless. All the kids rushed in to embrace Jesus. One by one, He blessed each child with a cuddle. He took babies from their mothers and blessed them too.

Hannah and her brothers worked their way out of the crowd and watched as Jesus blessed child after child. He was having a wonderful time.

"He said, the kingdom of God belongs to children," Hannah said. "What does that mean?"

"It means, kids rock!" James said. "Jesus loves kids."

"He sure does," Paul said. "But what Jesus actually said is that the kingdom of God belongs to people who are *like* children."

"What does that mean?" Hannah repeated.

"I think it means people need to desire Jesus the way kids do," Paul said.

"And they need to believe in Him like kids do too," James said.

Paul turned to look at James, "That's a better answer, I think. Kids just get Jesus. They love Him without question."

"Yeah," James agreed.

Hannah tugged on her brothers' arms, "Look!" She pointed as Jesus threw a little boy way up in the air and caught him. "I get so scared when Dad does that!"

Paul spoke, "I don't think Jesus would do it if He didn't know that He would catch him."

"If Jesus drops him," James said, "He can just heal him!"

"Right James, as if!" Paul laughed. "I don't think Jesus goes around hurting people so He can heal them!"

James laughed. "Yeah, you're probably right."

As Jesus blessed another child, a finely dressed man walked up to the crowd. The man worked his way through all the kids, knelt in front of Jesus, and asked, "Good Teacher, what must I do to have eternal life?"

Jesus smiled at the man and said, "You know the commandments:

'You must not murder. You must not commit adultery. You must not steal. You must not testify falsely. Love your neighbor as yourself. Honor your father and mother.'"

"Teacher," the man pointed at the children on the ground, "I've obeyed all these commandments since I was young."

Looking at the man, Jesus' face broke into a wide smile, and His eyes filled with tears. "There is still one thing you haven't done," Jesus told him. "Go and sell all your possessions and give the money to the poor, and you will have treasure in heaven. Then come, follow Me."

The man's hand fell to a money bag dangling from his belt. He squeezed it tightly without saying anything. His other hand formed a fist. He tried to speak but couldn't. He looked like he was going to cry. He relaxed his hands and brought them together in front of him, clasping them as if he were about to pray. Then, shaking his head, he stood and pushed his way back through the crowd.

Jesus watched as the man disappeared into the multitude of adults behind the crowd of children. Once the man was gone, Jesus looked up at His disciples who were standing nearby, holding kids who wanted to see Jesus. Jesus said to His disciples, "How hard it is for the rich to enter the kingdom of God!"

The disciples shot looks at each other. They didn't understand.

Then Jesus turned to the crowd of kids in front of Him and said, "Dear children, it is very hard to enter the kingdom of God. In fact, it is easier for a camel to go through the eye of a needle than for a rich person to enter the kingdom of God!"

The disciples were clearly upset by Jesus' words. "Then who in the world can be saved?" one disciple asked.

Jesus took His eyes off the children, looked intently at the disciples, and said, "Humanly speaking, it is impossible. But not with God—everything is possible with God."

Hannah looked at her brothers, "It must be really hard to get into heaven!"

The Kingdom Scroll

"That's not what Jesus said," Paul answered. "He just said you can't buy your way in."

"You've got to be like a kid," James said.

"Small like a kid?" Hannah asked. "Or what?"

"Humble like a child," Paul said. "Kids believe people. They trust people. They truly need others. Children go where adults take them."

"So," Hannah was trying to understand, "because we trust Jesus to take us to His kingdom, He does?"

"Exactly," James said. "I think Jesus meant that it is hard to get into God's kingdom if you are trying to get there."

"And rich people try to pay for everything," Hannah said. "And God's kingdom isn't for sale!"

"That's it!" James said. "She's got it, folks!"

The three kids laughed together. They watched Jesus with the children until all the kids were blessed. One by one, moms and dads gathered their little ones and left. When it had finally quieted down, a group of disciples told Jesus they had all been invited to Lazarus's house for dinner.

Jesus smiled, "Oh, I love Martha's cooking! Let's go." Jesus stood and followed His disciples. As they walked away, Jesus turned and gestured for the kids to follow. James saw it.

"Jesus just called us to follow Him," James said.

"Well, if we've learned anything—" Paul began.

Hannah interrupted, "We should follow Jesus!"

Kingdom Children

Thought Questions: Chapter 19
1. Why can Jesus see and touch the kids when no one else in the Bible can?
2. How is childlike faith different from grown-up faith? Why does Jesus like childlike faith?
3. Why did the rich man walk away sad instead of following Jesus?

Bible Adventurer Bonus:

You can read the story this chapter is based on in Matthew 19:13–26.

Chapter 20
One-Foot Law

After a short walk, Jesus and the disciples reached a house on the outskirts of town. As the disciples removed their shoes outside of the house, the kids hurried through the door and stood in a corner where they could see everything without feeling they were in the way.

As they entered the house, the disciples were greeted by a lovely lady. Each disciple said, "Good evening, Mary." And she returned the greeting, "Good evening, Peter. Good evening, Matthew. Good evening, Bartholomew. Good evening, John." She went through all twelve names before finishing, "Good evening, Jesus."

They sat on large pillows and leaned against the wall. Some of the disciples lay on the pillows rather than sitting. A couple of servants quickly busied themselves with washing the dust off of the men's feet.

"How many of their names can you remember?" Hannah whispered.

"Maybe five or six," James said. "What about you, Paul?"

Paul looked around the room and studied each face, muttering their names to himself as he did so. "I think I can name all of them."

"No way!" James laughed. "You've got a great memory!"

Hannah patted her big brother on the back. "You're smart."

"Thanks, Hannah," Paul said. "Now let's listen quietly, so we don't distract Jesus."

One-Foot Law

Once the disciples were all comfortable and clean, Martha entered with a platter of bread and dip. She put it in the middle of the table. Mary followed with a few large jugs of water.

"You know," one of the disciples said, "they say 'if these walls could talk.' Well, Martha cooks for so many people, I think in her house the phrase should be 'if these bowls and platters could talk!'"

A rush of laugher filled the room. Jesus lifted a piece of bread to His mouth as He laughed at Bartholomew's joke. "Yes, Bart," Jesus said, "Martha's dishes have many stories to tell."

"This platter will be back in the kitchen before it has a chance!" Peter said, as he stuffed two pieces of bread into his mouth at once, one with each hand. The group of disciples laughed uproariously.

"Where's the main course?" John quipped, "It is written, 'Man shall not live by bread alone!'"

Martha spoke up from the kitchen, "Well, John, you're too young to be called a man—you can't even grow a beard! So you can live on bread alone, boy!"

Guffaws, giggles, and snorts of merriment swept around the room.

"Oh, Johnny boy, she got you!" Bart said.

John shook his head, smiling. What comeback could there be to such a well-timed quip? The room quieted as the men enjoyed the bread and water.

"Jesus," John said after washing down another piece of bread, "why are people always trying to trick You? I mean, it's one thing to have humorous stabs at each other in good fun. But, it seems You get attacked from every angle by people who don't even know You."

"People mock what they don't understand," Jesus replied.

"Like this morning," John continued, "that law expert came out of his dungeon of scrolls and thought he was going to nail You to the wall with his question."

"Ah yes," Jesus answered, "he already knew the answer. They often do. It's the unfaced questions of the heart that really need asking."

"That's why You like to answer with stories, isn't it?" Bart interjected.

Jesus nodded, but Peter answered, "That story this morning—about the good Samaritan who outdid the Jewish leaders. That was great! You really sent that scholar running back to the safety of his books!"

Everyone laughed again. "It's true!" Bart shouted over the din, "Jesus' stories and questions put His critics on unsure footing! They either stumble away thunderstruck or just fade back into the crowd."

"And I hope they have been challenged to look at their hearts," Jesus said seriously.

The disciples focused on their Master. They had learned to recognize a teaching moment as it approached.

"They all want to minimize their effort and maximize their results," Jesus said. "And they are wise to do so. Life's purpose can only be achieved if we remove that which hinders and focus on that which draws the kingdom of God closer."

Silence filled the room as the disciples chewed on this spiritual wisdom. Finally, John spoke, "You told the expert in the law to be like the Samaritan. Is that the one thing we all must do?"

"Love your neighbor," Jesus said. "Yes, love wastefully. Sacrifice whatever it is that stands between you and your ability to help without hesitation."

Bart said, "Is that why, this afternoon, you challenged that rich guy to sell all his stuff and give the money to the poor?"

"Yes," Jesus said. "Imagine the lives he could bless by giving generously!"

"We've left everything behind to follow You," Peter said. "What reward is waiting for us in the kingdom?"

"Peter, you can have a throne," Jesus said with a laugh, "you all can." He lifted a cup of water, toasting them all, "Thrones all around."

The disciples laughed and cheered rowdily. The laughter died down quickly as they continued chewing on bread.

"But, that's not the point," John said thoughtfully. "Is it?"

One-Foot Law

Jesus was sipping from His cup. He raised His eyebrows in agreement. The room stilled, awaiting His response.

"What is written in the law?" Jesus replied. "How do you read it?"

The disciples went quiet. No one was brave enough to answer Jesus' question.

"You know the answer," Jesus said. "It is too easy. That's why you do not attempt putting it into words. What is the point of the law and of life? What does the kingdom of God require of you?"

The silence deepened.

Jesus stood. "You have all heard of Rabbi Hillel, who used to teach at the synagogue in Jerusalem?"

The disciples nodded. Rabbi Hillel was a well-known scholar who died while the disciples were children.

"Rabbi Hillel was once challenged by a young skeptic," Jesus said. "The young man said, 'You want me to believe in your God? Fine. I will believe, if you can recite the entire Torah while standing on one foot!'"

A few of the disciples snickered.

"The entire Torah?" Bart questioned. "That's Genesis, Exodus, Leviticus, Numbers, and Deuteronomy—five books!"

John said, "There's no way anyone could stand on one foot that long, even if he did have the entire Torah memorized."

"Well, Rabbi Hillel wasn't just anyone!" Jesus said, as He lifted one foot in the air and rested it on His knee. Balancing on one foot, Jesus said, "Rabbi Hillel lifted his foot off the ground and said, 'Whatever is hateful to you, do not do to your neighbor. This is the whole Torah. The rest is just details. Go and study it for yourself!'" Jesus stomped His foot, as if crushing a bug.

The disciples broke into rowdy applause.

"That was an awesome answer," Paul said during the cheering.

James nodded, "It sure was!"

Hannah took the hands of both of her brothers. "This is so much fun!" she whispered as the cheering died down.

Sitting on His pillow again, Jesus said, "I hope each of you always remembers the value God places on each and every person. Rabbi Hillel may have said not to do what is hateful, but people who seek the kingdom of God will go even further."

"What more is there?" John asked.

"Do," Jesus said. "Don't just 'not do' things that hurt others. *Do!* Imagine the best thing that could ever happen to you; then go do that thing for your neighbor! Do to others what you wish they would do to you."

The disciples nodded. "That makes a lot of sense, Jesus," Bart said. "To live in the kingdom of God we must treat people the way God would treat them."

"Yes," Jesus said, clapping His hands together. "Yes! Be the hands and feet of God. Be God's mouthpiece. Live with God's heart inside of you. Take God's kingdom to the world!"

Thought Questions: Chapter 20
1. Why is this chapter called "One-Foot Law"? What does it mean?
2. Why is loving others the most important thing in the law of the kingdom of God?
3. Who does it change when we love others? How?

Bible Adventurer Bonus:

You can read the story this chapter is based on

in Luke 10:25–38.

Chapter 21
God's Storyteller

Jesus and the disciples continued talking, eating, and laughing late into the night. Paul, James, and Hannah sat cross-legged in the corner and listened with rapt fascination. It was amazing to be able to see how much the disciples respected Jesus and how much He loved them. They were the best of friends.

Hannah turned to her brothers and whispered, "All night, I've been wondering something."

"Really?" James said, "Why didn't you just ask us?"

"I dunno," Hannah answered, "I just like thinking about everything."

"What have you been wondering?" Paul asked, interested.

Hannah stopped braiding a strand of hair and let it fall to her shoulder. "Why did Jesus call it the kingdom of God rather than the family of God?"

James answered first, "Because Jesus didn't come to earth to play house!"

Hannah crossed her little arms in frustration. "I'm serious, James. We are all God's children. We are His family. Why didn't Jesus call His people 'family'? He's always saying kingdom this and kingdom that!"

Paul put his hand on his sister's knee. "I think James is on the right track. Jesus wants people to imagine a world where God is King and what it would be like to live in that world."

The Kingdom Scroll

"Why not imagine God as their Father?" Hannah asked.

"Well, Jesus did call God His Father," Paul said slowly, thinking about his answer.

James took advantage of Paul's silence. "If I lived in a kingdom like Nebuchadnezzar's, where the king was selfish and demanded worship, I would love to hear Jesus talk about a kingdom where everyone loved each other—and where the king loved them!"

"Right on!" Paul said, amazed at his younger brother. "You've got it, James. Jesus wanted people to know they could live in God's kingdom—a kingdom of love—even while their nation was being ruled by an evil king. Jesus was giving them a new way to live by giving them a new king and kingdom."

"That makes sense," Hannah said.

Suddenly, Paul interrupted his sister. "Hey, there's another line on the scroll card!"

"That was quick," James said.

"What does it say?" Hannah asked.

"It says"—Paul held the card in front of himself—" 'Kingdom Stories.' "

"I love stories!" Hannah clapped her hands. "Let's go."

The three children pointed their fingers and touched the card. Immediately, the world around them went white.

"Let's guess where we are," Paul said.

"Are there children in this story?" Hannah asked.

The sound of children's voices came from behind them. Seconds later, two boys ran past. "I hope He tells lots of stories!" one yelled, as they jogged past. "I hope He heals people," the other said, as they ran.

"This must be one of the days when Jesus heals people and tells stories," Paul said in an even tone.

The three kids sat, still in the same position, under a tree in a field of dry grass. Just above the horizon, the sun began to warm the crisp morning air. At the bottom of the slope of the field in which they sat, a beautiful lake spread into the distance, the sun glimmering off the rippling water. A boat, sailing on the lake, was coming toward the beach below them.

"Jesus is on that boat," James said. "That's why it appeared when you said His name. When they land, lots of people will gather for healing and stories."

Paul nudged his siblings and pointed behind them to the top of the hill where the running boys had come from. A huge crowd crested the hill and descended toward them. "You said, 'lots of people.'" Paul laughed.

The three watched as the crowd of people separated around them and the tree they were sitting under and walked toward the water. The people sat in clusters on the ground. More people poured over the hilltop. The entire field filled with people.

Jesus climbed out of the boat and started working his way through the crowd, stopping at each group to heal their sick and tell stories. When He got close to the large tree, someone shouted, "Tell us about the kingdom of God!"

Jesus paused and then said, "How can I describe the kingdom of God? What story should I use to illustrate it?" He stroked his beard for a few seconds as He scanned the crowd standing near Him. Suddenly, He smiled and threw His hand up as an idea struck Him.

Jesus swept His hand across the once-empty field, now filled with people. "The kingdom of God is like a farmer who scatters seed on the ground. Night and day, while he's asleep or awake, the seed sprouts and grows, but he does not understand how it happens. The earth produces the crops on its own."

Jesus put His hand on the head of a small girl standing in front of Him and looked down at her smiling face. "First, a leaf blade pushes through the rough ground."

Jesus gestured with both hands to a group of unmarried teenage girls sitting in the shade of the tree. "Then the heads of wheat are formed."

Next he pointed to a man who had his arm draped over the shoulder

The Kingdom Scroll

of his heavily pregnant wife. "And finally the grain ripens. And as soon as the grain is ready . . ."

Jesus turned and swept His hands over the massive crowd between the tree and the water's edge, "The farmer comes and harvests it with a sickle, for the harvest time has come."

Every cluster of people began talking at once. Jesus had just given them a lot to discuss!

"Jesus is such a good storyteller," Hannah said.

"He sure is," Paul said. "I wish He were a teacher at our school!"

"That would be awesome!" James agreed. "I could listen to His stories all day."

"Yeah," Paul said distractedly. "Hey, look at this! That funny symbol has appeared again on the scroll card."

James became quiet and his full attention snapped back to the card. "You're right! That means we are all going to different stories!"

"Be very careful to notice where you leave your footprints," Paul said. "We want to have fun this time and not feel scared and lost!"

"I want to see the footprints this time," Hannah said. "I'm going to move around on this trip."

"Let's go," James said. "I'm so excited!"

"OK," Paul said, holding the card steady in front of himself. "Fingers out!"

Three hands reached toward the card, fingers extended, and touched in unison.

James and Hannah disappeared with a popping sound. Paul stood, holding the scroll card, just as he had been a moment before. The crowd of people still sat in the field. The big tree still stood where it had been.

"I didn't go anywhere." Paul said, confused. Then he noticed something odd. The people were not talking. They weren't even moving. They were frozen.

Thought Questions: Chapter 21

1. How can we live in God's kingdom right now?
2. Describe what each of these terms make you think of: *God's family, God's army, God's church.*
3. Jesus talked a lot about God's kingdom. Why? Why didn't He use the terms listed in questions 2? What did He want us to know about God and His place in our world?

Bible Adventurer Bonus:

You can read the stories this chapter is based on in Mark 4:26–30.

Chapter 22
Kingdom Stories

Paul stared at the hundreds of statue people. Then he heard a splash from behind him.

Spinning around, he saw that the boat was farther out in the water and was filled with busy fishermen. They threw a massive net as far as they could and waited for it to sink into the water.

Then the captain yelled, "Pull!" And they began to pull the ropes to drag the net to the surface. The men struggled. They pulled with all of their might. But they didn't seem to be able to budge the net.

The captain leaned over the side of the boat, peering into the water. He yelled, "Hold! It's full!" The men stopped pulling and held fast. Two men leaped over the side and tied the ropes tightly under their arms. Then they held on to the side of the boat. Another two men jumped in and did the same. Soon all the men were in the water.

Together they dragged the net to the shore right in front of Paul. As the men got to the water's edge, they turned and pulled the net out of the water and onto the beach. Paul couldn't believe how full the net was. It was bulging with thrashing, flopping fish.

The captain sailed the little boat toward shore, running it aground in the soft sand. He walked to the bow of the boat, holding two large crates. He held the crates out and shouted over the heads of the men,

"You there! Come take these crates!"

Paul spun to see who was behind him. There was no one. A fisherman let go of his rope and headed toward the captain. The captain shouted at the man, "Don't loosen your rope until the net is completely on shore!" The young fisherman clearly thought the captain had been talking to him.

"I'm talking to you, boy!" The captain looked at Paul. "You'll never become a fisherman if you can't obey a captain. Get over here and take these crates!"

Paul spun around and looked behind himself again. There was no way the captain could see him. Paul knew that. But there was no one else. Certainly, there was no other boy!

"Quit looking around like a stunned mullet!" the captain chided. "You act like you're invisible or something!" The captain's tone turned dark, "Get over here and take these crates!"

Paul moved into action. He didn't understand it, but he hated getting in trouble. He ran to the captain, waded into the water, and took the two crates.

"Good boy," the captain said. "Line them up behind the men. And be quick about it, there's more to be set out!"

Paul ran the crates back to the men and set each crate behind a different fisherman. Then he returned to the captain, who was waiting with two more crates. After a few trips, the crates were all set out and Paul was tired. He rested his hands on his knees and took a few deep breaths.

The men were pulling all different kinds of fish out of the net. Paul watched as the men put the big healthy fish in the crates and chucked the small or sickly fish back into the water.

When the sorting was finished and the net was empty, the men froze in position. The fish stopped flapping. The water on the shoreline stopped lapping.

Paul looked around and realized everything had completely stopped.

The parable must be over, he thought. *What just happened? That captain could see me. I guess that means the men could too. How weird!*

Paul walked to where he had been standing when the parable started. He saw his own footprints embedded deeply in the sand.

He stepped into them.

* * * * *

James stood in the middle of a small kitchen. A wooden table in front of him was covered with a thin layer of white powder. A water jug sat next to the powdered area. He touched the white powder and held it up to his nose. It smelled safe, so he put it to his tongue.

"Flour," James said out loud.

"Of course, it's flour," a stern voice said from behind him. James's heart nearly leaped out of his chest. He twisted around and saw a woman wearing an apron holding out a wooden bowl filled with flour.

"I'm not going to stand here all day," the woman said. "Take it!"

James was so confused that he did as he was told. He took the bowl and stood staring at the woman. His mouth opened to say something then closed. He was completely at a loss for words. *How can she see me?* he thought. *And hear me?*

The woman turned and grabbed a pinch of something from a little jar. She dropped the pinch into the bowl. "There, just a pinch of leaven. OK, work your magic." She looked up at James.

He stared back, agog.

"Don't just stand there," the woman said, putting her hands on her hips. "Put it on the tabletop and knead it!"

James spun around, still in shock, and set the bowl next to the jug of water. The woman walked around the table and poured the water into the bowl. She thrust her hands into the bowl, saying, "Do I have to do everything for you? You'll never learn if you don't get your hands dirty!" She pulled the rough lump of dough out of the bowl and tossed it at James.

Instinctively, he caught it. Now he knew what the layer of flour was for—it would keep the dough from sticking to the table. He began punching and rolling, punching and rolling—kneading the dough until it had a smooth texture. He worked hard as his mind raced. *She really can see me!*

He stopped and looked at the dough. The woman lifted it and stretched it. She smiled. "Well done," she said. "Now we'll just put it back in the bowl and let it rise. It's amazing what a little leaven can do!" She lifted the dough, dropped it into the bowl, and placed a towel over it. As the towel settled on the bowl, the woman stood, silently staring at the bowl.

James waited for her to say something else. She didn't.

"How can you see me?" James asked.

The woman continued staring at the bowl without answering.

"Can you hear me?" James said, leaning toward the woman.

She didn't move.

James studied her more closely. She didn't seem to be breathing. He waved his hand in front of her face.

She didn't flinch.

"She's frozen!" James said more to himself than anyone else.

He took a step away from the bench and felt his foot slip in a hole. He stumbled backward and looked down just as his other foot dropped into a similar shaped hole.

"They're my footprints," he realized, just a second too late.

Thought Questions: Chapter 22

1. Why do you think these people can see, hear, and interact with the kids?
2. What do the fish represent in Paul's story?
3. What is the lesson in James's story?

Bible Adventurer Bonus:

You can read the parables this chapter is based on in Matthew 13:33, 47–49.

Chapter 23
Hidden Treasure

Hannah looked from side to side, exploring her new surroundings.

It wasn't completely new. Her brothers had disappeared and so had the lake. But there was still a field with a big tree in it.

Then she noticed a man leading a donkey and a cart past the tree. Suddenly, he tripped. The donkey stopped in surprise. The man turned around and looked at the ground. The man knelt down and began examining the ground. Then he started pulling up clumps of grass and throwing them aside.

"Weird," Hannah said. "Let's go see what he's doing." She took a couple of steps and then stopped, remembering. She turned and examined her footprints. They were sunk into the ground next to a boulder. "I think I can find them again," she said and then ran to where the man was digging.

When she arrived, the man had completely removed the grass from a big square of ground. A loop of metal was sticking up from the middle of the square.

The man looked up from his digging and said, "Can you grab a shovel from my cart?"

Hannah looked behind her to see who the man was talking to.

Sitting against the trunk of the tree was a girl about Hannah's age.

The Kingdom Scroll

"Sure, Daddy," she replied. Then she jumped up and ran to the cart. Soon she came around the other side of the donkey, carrying a shovel. "Here, Daddy."

"Thanks, honey," the man said and took the shovel. He started digging with quick strokes. After watching the man dig for bit, Hannah looked up at the girl. She smiled. Hannah turned to look behind her. There was no one there. Hannah looked back at the girl. She was still smiling. Hannah was sure she had seen the girl before. *She looks just like—*

The man let out a whoop of joy as he dusted off the cover of an old chest. His daughter looked down. "What is it, Daddy?"

"Let's have a look," he said, as he slowly lifted the lid. The chest opened toward Hannah and blocked her view of the man. All she could see was the lid and the reaction on the little girl's face. "Oh, Daddy! It's beautiful! Can we take it?"

"Not yet," the man said, "but we will!" He quickly covered the chest with dirt and rushed back to the donkey. "Come on, Roseanne, we've got a field to buy!"

A chill ran up Hannah's spine. When the man called his daughter Roseanne, Hannah knew exactly where she had seen the girl before.

She looks just like my imaginary friend who appears only in my bedroom, Hannah thought. The weird thing was that her imaginary friend, who looked just like this girl, was also named Roseanne. And nobody knew about her. Nobody!

The man, donkey, and cart moved away from the tree. As the cart passed Hannah, Roseanne was sitting on the back, her feet swinging. She smiled, patted the space next to her on the cart, and called out, "Come on, Hannah!"

Hannah threw her hand over her mouth in surprise. "It is Roseanne!" she giggled. Then she ran with all of her strength to catch up with the cart.

The next few hours went by quickly for Hannah. She and Roseanne

Hidden Treasure

had a wonderful time talking about everything the cart went past. There were flowers, goats, people working in fields, women getting water from a well, and cobblestone roads in the town.

Roseanne's Dad stopped the cart for quite a while in town and went into a building. He said it was a landlord's office. He came back out after an hour or so with a few bags filled with coins. He handed them to Roseanne. "Hide these under your dress, Rosie dear," he said. "We've got to go talk to the man who owns the field."

They drove out of town and turned some time later at a large property with a beautiful, long track lined with huge trees that formed a canopy above the road. The man stopped the cart in front of a large homestead. He came to the back of the cart, got the bags from Roseanne, and went inside. It wasn't long and he was back with a piece of paper.

He unrolled it and showed it to the girls. "Look at that, ladies." He smiled at Hannah, "We've got ourselves a field!"

"And a treasure chest," Roseanne whispered.

The man put his finger over his lips, *Shhhh*. He smiled a happy smile. "Let's go explore our field!"

The cart began moving again and stopped a few minutes later under the tree where it had started. Hannah and Roseanne hopped off the cart.

The man came to the back and grabbed the shovel. He handed the rolled up paper to Roseanne. "Rosie, dear, you hold this for Daddy." He was nearly laughing with joy, "You and your friend can have a look at it while I change our future!"

The man led the donkey to the patch of bare dirt and positioned the cart in such a way that it would be ready for the chest. Then he started digging. He talked while he worked, "I've sold everything, Rosie, dear: the house, the farm, the horses, and the goats. All we have left is the donkey and the cart." He paused and, then with a grunt of effort, lifted the chest out of the ground and carried it over to the girls, "And a little box of goodies!"

The Kingdom Scroll

Roseanne laughed and clapped her hands with glee. "Can we look inside, Daddy?"

"Of course," he said, placing the treasure chest on the cart. "Let's have a look. Climb up here." He held his hand down to Roseanne. Once she was in the cart, he reached down to Hannah. She took his hand and was soon standing next to Roseanne in the cart.

The man took one side of the chest and gestured to the girls to grab the other side. They lifted the lid together and the treasure inside was fully revealed.

Hannah was amazed. There were chains of gold, rubies, emeralds, and just about every other kind of precious stone and metal she could imagine. She waited for the man to reach into the treasure chest. But he just stared at the wonders before him. She turned to Roseanne. She, too, was staring intently at the treasure.

Nobody moved for a long time. Finally, Hannah stepped back and examined the other two. They were not just standing still—they were like statues. They were frozen. "Story's over," Hannah said out loud. "How weird!"

She got down off the cart and walked back to the stone near her footprints. She found them easily. She stood behind her footprints and then stepped into them, one at a time.

Hidden Treasure

Thought Questions: Chapter 23
1. What would be in a treasure chest filled with your favorite things?
2. Do you have an imaginary friend? Why do you think Roseanne is in this story?
3. How did Hannah know the story was over? Why did this happen?

Bible Adventurer Bonus:

You can read the parable this chapter is based on in Matthew 13:44.

"Jesus always used stories and illustrations like these when speaking to the crowds. In fact, he never spoke to them without using such parables. This fulfilled the prophecy that said,

" 'I will speak to you in parables.
I will explain mysteries hidden since the creation of the world' " (Matthew 13:34, 35, NLT).

Chapter 24
God's Kingdom

All three kids pulled their finger away from the kingdom scroll card and looked up at each other with excitement.

"How awesome was that?" James said, falling backward onto the sandy beach.

Paul and Hannah sat down, cross-legged in front of James, forming a circle.

Paul glanced over at the boat. The captain and his fishermen were gone. Jesus and His disciples sat in the boat. People waded around in the water, having fun.

"Could people see you in your story?" Paul asked.

"Yes!" both Hannah and James answered together.

"I made bread," James said, "with a really bossy lady!"

"I carried crates for a fishing captain," Paul said, "while the fishermen separated the good fish from the bad."

"I went on a cart ride," Hannah said, "with my imaginary friend."

The boys both stared at her, thinking she was joking.

"You what?" James asked. "Your imaginary what?"

"Nobody knows about Roseanne," Hannah said. "She's only in my bedroom. Well, until now. Evidently, she's in the Bible too."

"That explains it!" Paul said with a laugh.

God's Kingdom

"Explains what?" James said, staring at his brother. "I'm more confused than ever. How could that woman see me and hear me? And what is Hannah's imaginary friend doing in the Bible?"

"Exactly," Paul said, clapping his hands. "Imaginary!"

"Please explain," James said, sitting up.

Paul looked at Hannah, "First, Hannah, tell us what Bible story you were actually in."

Hannah said, "It was the story where Jesus says a man found a treasure in a field, sold all his stuff, and bought the field so he could have the treasure."

"Ah," Paul said, nodding his head. "Yes!"

James was completely anxious now. "*Tell us!* What do you know?"

"Two things," Paul said.

Hannah pulled her knees up under her chin and hugged them as she listened to Paul. James's hands were in fists, driving into his folded knees.

"First," Paul said, "we could interact with the people because they were in parables."

"Why does that matter?" James asked.

"Parables are fictional," Paul said. "They are imaginary stories from the mind of Jesus."

"And?" James asked.

"Fictional stories are created by the listener as well as the teller."

"So," James was starting to understand, "we were creating part of the parable ourselves?"

"Only the part that wasn't in the real parable," Paul said. "The real story line and point are still intact."

"We are just adding our bits," Hannah said. "The people and things we would like to be in the story."

"Yes," Paul said. "James and I wanted to be involved. So we became involved."

"What about me?" Hannah asked.

"You wanted to have a friend with you," Paul said.

123

The Kingdom Scroll

"And Roseanne appeared." Hannah clapped her hands. "That's awesome!"

James was still thinking it through. "You said there were two things you realized. What's the second one?"

"All three of our stories had the same point," Paul said.

"No way," James argued. "You're just wrong on that one."

"Yeah," Hannah added. "How can finding treasure, making bread, and counting fish all have the same point?"

"All three, when Jesus told them as parables," Paul said, "start with the same key words."

"They do?" both Hannah and James said together.

"Yes," Paul said. "The kingdom of heaven is like . . ."

"Whoa," James said. "That's neat. So, they are all kingdom stories?"

"Yes," Paul said. "Let's think about what each story teaches us about God's kingdom. Mine is easy, God chooses who goes to heaven by separating the good and bad at the end of time."

Hannah said, "Yeah, mine is easy too. God's kingdom is like an awesome treasure. Once you discover it, you will happily give up anything and everything in order to make it yours."

James scratched his head for a minute. The other two looked at him, waiting. "Well," he said, "it was hard work making bread. But I don't think that's the point of the story."

"Did anything unique happen in the story," Paul asked.

"She made me hold the bowl while she put something small in," James said. "I don't even know what it was. It sounded like *heaven*. Oh yeah, leaven. What's that?"

"Yeast," Paul said.

"I know what yeast is," Hannah said excitedly. "It makes bread rise. Without it, you get flat bread!"

"And she only put a little bit in?" Paul asked.

"That's all you need," Hannah said. "A little bit of yeast goes a long way!"

God's Kingdom

"That's what she said," James remembered. "The woman said, 'It's amazing what a little leaven can do!'"

"So," Paul asked, "what does it teach us about the kingdom of God?"

"Well," James said, "the leaven of heaven goes a long way. If the kingdom of God gets into you even a little bit, it will have a huge impact on your life."

"I like that—the leaven of heaven," Paul said.

"We've learned a lot about God's kingdom," Hannah said.

"I didn't even mean to learn," James said with a smile. "It was just so much fun!"

Paul pulled out the scroll card. All three kids looked at it with a sense of relief and disappointment. There on the bottom, in bold black letters, were the words *The End*.

"Shall we?" Paul asked.

"Yup," Hannah said. "Home sounds good!"

Three hands, fingers extended, reached forward and touched the card.

In a flash, they were standing back in the boys' room. They all studied the room as if it were a foreign place.

"It's so weird, being back here so suddenly," James said.

"I know," Paul said, looking at the Bible on his desk. "We were just in there!"

"I wish we could stay in the Bible forever," Hannah said.

"It was fun," James said, grabbing his Rubik's Cube off the desk. "But, I love being in the real world too."

"We shouldn't love the world," Hannah said. "It's a bad place!"

Paul added, "Yeah, the Bible says the world is evil, and we should stay away from evil."

James twisted a couple of sides on the cube. "God loved the world enough to let His Son die for it," he said. "If God loved the world that much, I think we should love it too."

Just then, Dad walked into the room.

Before Dad could say anything, Paul asked, "Dad, doesn't the Bible say we should be 'in the world but not of the world'?"

Dad nodded his head, but before he could answer, James blurted, "What does that even mean, 'In but not of'?"

Hannah asked, "When Jesus said, 'God so loved the world' did He mean only the people or the whole entire world and everything in it?"

Everyone stared at Hannah in befuddled wonder. So she explained herself, "I mean, couldn't Jesus have said, 'God so loved the people of earth that He sent His Son'? If that's what He meant."

Dad crossed the room and lifted his little girl into his arms, "Hannah, that is a very powerful thought," Dad said. "There is no doubt that God loves everything He made. And He did make everything living on the earth—"

James interrupted, " 'In but not of'? I'm still lost back at 'in but not of.' " He banged the Rubik's Cube into his forehead a few times. "Earth to James. Earth to James. 'In but not of.' "

Everyone laughed.

"James, you are too much," Paul said.

Dad sat on the bed, holding Hannah on his lap. "I think Hannah just gave us the answer," Dad said. "God loves everything and everyone He made. And, if we want to be like Him, we must love them too."

"So," James said, "we should love what God loves?"

"Precisely," Dad said. "Jesus said we should love others the same way we love ourselves!"

"Hey, that's what God said after giving the Ten Commandments," Paul said. "Love the Lord your God with all your heart, soul, and strength. And love your neighbor as yourself."

"That's what it means to be like Jesus," Dad said. "If we love others, God's kingdom is not far from any one of us."

"God's kingdom is a like treasure," Hannah said. "It's more valuable than anything else!"

"And it's like yeast," James said, locking eyes with Dad. "A little bit

God's Kingdom

of it changes our whole life!"

"It sure does," Dad said, smiling at his three kids. "You are amazing kids. Did you know that?"

They all smiled.

"We learned so many stories about the kingdom of God," Hannah said.

"It was awesome," James added. "We saw statues, stones, and stories!"

"Can we tell you all the stories we saw and heard?" Hannah asked, wrapping her arms around Dad's neck.

"That would be great," Dad said. "Let's go sit on the couch and get comfortable. I want to hear every detail in your story of God's kingdom!"

Thought Questions: Chapter 24
1. Would you like to go inside of a parable? Why? Which one would you choose?
2. What have you learned about the kingdom of God in this book?
3. The kids' Dad said, "If we love others, God's kingdom is not far from any one of us." What did he mean? How can we live in God's kingdom every day?

Bible Adventurer Bonus:

Jesus said, "So now I am giving you a new commandment: Love each other. Just as I have loved you, you should love each other. Your love for one another will prove to the world that you are my disciples" (John 13:34, NLT).

MORE ADVENTURES IN THE BIBLE

The Lamb Scroll

by David Edgren

In book two of the Adventures in the Bible trilogy, Paul, James, and Hannah discover the Lamb through the stories in the Bible. Challenged to dig deeply into the Word, they learn to forgive, find the answers to some difficult questions, and realize that even children are called to be disciples.

Paperback, 128 pages
ISBN 13: 978-0-8163-2375-3
ISBN 10: 0-8163-2375-5

The Serpent Scroll

by David Edgren

Book one of the Adventures in the Bible trilogy takes Paul, James, and Hannah on an exciting adventure through several books of the Bible and introduces them to using a concordance. As the children "travel" through the Bible, they discover that the stories are all linked together, from Genesis to Revelation.

Paperback, 128 pages
ISBN 13: 978-0-8163-2330-2
ISBN 10: 0-8163-2330-5

Pacific Press® Publishing Association
"Where the Word Is Life"

Three ways to order:

1	Local	Adventist Book Center®
2	Call	1-800-765-6955
3	Shop	AdventistBookCenter.com